TRACKING
WONDER

Reclaiming a Life of Meaning
and Possibility in a World
Obsessed with Productivity

JEFFREY DAVIS

sounds true

BOULDER, COLORADO

Sounds True
Boulder, CO 80306

Published 2021

Cover design by Jennifer Miles
Book design by Linsey Dodaro

The wood used to produce this book is from
Forest Stewardship Council (FSC) certified forests,
recycled materials, or controlled wood.

Printed in the United States of America

BK06075

Library of Congress Cataloging-in-Publication Data

Names: Davis, Jeffrey, author.
Title: Tracking wonder : reclaiming a life of meaning and possibility
in a
   world obsessed with productivity / by Jeffrey Davis.
Description: Boulder, CO : Sounds True, 2022.
Identifiers: LCCN 2021018282 (print) | LCCN 2021018283 (ebook) |
ISBN
   9781683646884 (hardback) | ISBN 9781683646891 (ebook)
Subjects: LCSH: Curiosity. | Possibility. | Meaning (Psychology)
Classification: LCC BF323.C8 D38 2022 (print) | LCC BF323.C8
(ebook) |
   DDC 155.2--dc23
LC record available at https://lccn.loc.gov/2021018282
LC ebook record available at https://lccn.loc.gov/2021018283

10 9 8 7 6 5 4 3 2 1

To Hillary, you've believed in this endeavor from the beginning.

To Dahlia and Alethea, you're my daily reminders of why I do what I do.

To Mom, you saw my young genius in all the ways it needed to be seen.

CONTENTS

INTRODUCTION

THE DAWN OF POSSIBILITY

TO EXPERIENCE WONDER IS our birthright—especially in times of challenge and change. In a fleeting moment with rippling effects, wonder can transfix us with the elegant design of a coat hook or the massive wafer of a harvest moon. It can help us delight in a mathematical insight or the surprising eloquence of a six-year-old child. For wonder is the one human experience that dissolves our biases so we can see the beauty of ourselves, one another, and our world more clearly. Wonder cracks us open to the beauty of this one life amid rampant uncertainty. But how does it do so—and what gets in our way with wonder?

Mornings can brim with possibility, afterall. Sunlight breaks the dark sky, your eyes open onto the ceiling, and you might wonder, "What could I experience *today*?" Maybe you imagine the ways your hours could unfold so that by night you felt you'd had a meaningful adventure. Yet, maybe your mind simply starts fretting about that unanswered email from your colleague or your child's lost retainer that exhausted your budget.

I begin the first hours of almost every morning with both minds. One is a summer camper who relishes the idea of mornings because I equate them with open opportunity to make the most of the day. I've been known to ask my family to join me in impromptu dance parties at breakfast, sometimes to their grumbling annoyance. As a result, even on a gray winter's morn, the inner light of our family amps up a few watts. Yet I also have a nervous Piglet mind. Even before I get out of bed, tiny worries can hijack huge amounts of mental megabytes that threaten to fritter away my energy. To waste time with constant worry seems like a petty crime to me. I'd rather expire at the end of a day with my pockets stuffed with wonder.

Wonder? Yes, even as a bespectacled, silver-haired man weighted down with responsibilities, I say *wonder*. Let me say this to you from the outset: Wonder is not simply for kids. Wonder is also radical grown-up stuff. It's for you, too.

Wonder is not simply for kids. Wonder is also radical grown-up stuff.

This book begins with this simple premise: when we look at visionaries, artists, scientists, and inspirational figures, we see that some of them have indeed practiced the proverbial ten thousand hours or demonstrated remarkable grit and focus in order to manifest their great work and fulfilled lives. But even more of them have a surprising advantage: they've kept alive an abiding sense of wonder. We now have increasing scientific evidence that experiences of wonder play a big role in sparking innovation, motivating us, and allowing us to derive meaning from what we create and experience.

The good news is that we all have access to this capacity to wonder. We always have. We just forget. Tracking wonder is the approach I have developed and tested so you can learn again how to reclaim a life of meaning and possibility without burning out. For as you will discover and as this book argues, wonder offers a beautiful counterbeat to our culture's obsessive drumbeat of productivity.

Imagine wonder as a multifaceted prism through which you can see and experience your days anew. In this book, we explore six such facets of wonder. Track wonder through each of its facets and you can live more creatively, deepen your relationships, and navigate surprising challenges with more flexibility.

The science, stories, and invitations I share here allow you to sharpen your understanding of wonder's dimensions and, if you choose, to apply them toward advancing an endeavor (personal, business, or otherwise) *creatively*.

Tracking wonder, then, is in part another form of paying attention. Maybe you've tried to "app your way to happiness" by downloading a dozen apps to help you meditate, measure your steps, and calculate your calories, all before 10:00 a.m. For some people, these methods are tremendously helpful. But many people are unsettled by messages of "Crush it!" "Hack your productivity!" and the incessant command to "Get things done!" If that sounds familiar, yet you're still looking to boost your creativity and find more fulfillment, you might benefit from experiencing wonder's facets.

Or perhaps you have a steady meditation or mindfulness practice but find that it doesn't give you the clarity and agency you're craving. A dose of wonder could be the missing ingredient of your practice that helps you foster a wholly new relationship with your mind. Tracking wonder every day in fact could help you measure the real value and beauty in your life.

THE HEART OF LIVING CREATIVELY

If you ever doubt your own creative potential, you're not alone. Over two-thirds of Americans believe creativity is valuable to our world, and a solid 75 percent value their own creativity in addressing personal and professional challenges, yet only one in four believes they are living up to their own creative potential.

Part of the problem is we sometimes get creativity all wrong. We don't view ourselves as creative or as leading fulfilling creative lives because we misunderstand what creativity is. When we talk about "creative" here, I mean creative in the sense of *how* you handle the inevitable uncertainties, doubts, and challenges in your life. *Creative* is not something reserved only for artists. *Creative* refers to how you can bring your ideas to fruition. What if the surprising advantage to living a life rich with creative possibility, meaning, and mastery is something we *all* have access to? What if each of us could shape such a life, no matter our circumstances?

In this age, your ability to fulfill your creative potential has less to do with developing a single-track talent in a specific domain and more to do with how you finesse challenges in pursuit of your aims. And as we'll see, it turns out that tracking experiences of wonder is the ideal skill set to do so.

RIPPLES OF WONDER

Imagine an experience of wonder like a pebble dropped into the pond of your perception. These moments, often quiet and fleeting, make ripples that expand and linger. Attend to enough of these rippling moments over time and your overall outlook just might shift for the better. What are some of those rippling effects?

Wonder is what can nudge your most meaningful ideas toward fulfillment even amid inevitable challenges: a computer crash, the toddler tantrum, or your own mental fatigue. Wonder, as we will see, also can provide the perspective to push through difficult experiences of grief, illness, or failure. For unlike almost any other emotional experience, wonder can keep us buoyant amid waves of uncertainty, sorrow, and fear without sinking into complete despair.

That's because wonder momentarily dissolves our habitual ways of seeing, relating, and thinking so we can glimpse again what is real and true, beautiful and possible. Consider what the English poet William Blake said about our perception: "If the doors of perception were cleansed everything would appear to man as it is, infinite. For man has closed himself up, till he sees all things through narrow chinks of his cavern." We each are wired to see things through narrow caverns for survival, but we human beings also have this extraordinary ability to trip our wiring with wonder and cleanse our perception.

Wonder also is a healing force. It snaps us out of cynicism and disbelief. It interrupts patterns of negativity, rumination, and monotony; rescues us from maelstroms or downward spirals; and offers us glimpses of another reality, right where we are. In addition, wonder turns us away from self-absorption and attunes us to others. People who experience wonder with each other develop strong bonds. Martha Nussbaum, a renowned theorist of ethics at the University of Chicago, says wonder is responsible for giving rise to other emotions—compassion, empathy, and love—that draw us out of ourselves and toward others. Experiencing more wonder can open us up to the folks we deem "different" from us. Wonder can favorably tip our emotional and psychological scales in areas such as generosity, optimism, and making a difference in other people's lives.

In part because of wonder's unique and subtle effects, René Descartes called wonder "the first of all the passions," while Socrates said that "philosophy [or the study of wisdom] begins in wonder." Wonder is with us from our first morning in this world and stays with us until the last. This book invites you to open up to it again for the dawns in between.

Tracking wonder and its six facets offer three avenues to help you fulfill your dreams:

LIVE MORE CREATIVELY. Through tracking wonder you can frame every day as a creative quest directed by your curiosity and insight. You can trace your unique force of character that has been with you since your best childhood days and that guides you toward your most fulfilling activities.

BUILD YOUR RESILIENCE. Tracking wonder shows you how to "fertilize confusion" when you're bewildered and how to find hope amid adversity—all as opportunities for creative, personal, and spiritual growth.

DEEPEN YOUR RELATIONSHIPS. Tracking wonder shows you how to dissolve your unconscious judgments, open up your mind so you can develop deeper connections, and practice the art of admiration.

And let's remember this: As anyone who has ever gazed up at the stars on a clear night knows, wonder is ultimately inexplicable, connecting us to the divine mysteries of the universe. It reminds us humbly that the more knowledge we gain, the more we discover we do not know.

WHERE I COME FROM AND WHERE YOU MIGHT COME FROM

To guide your tracking wonder journey as clearly as possible, I write from my singular perspective. I'm a cis male of European ethnic heritage residing in the Hudson Valley of New York. I'm neither wealthy nor poor, and don't experience disadvantage or discrimination regularly, if at all. I am well supported by my family, and I have been able to overcome hardships in part because of their help and love, as well as because of the tracking wonder practices I will share with you. I grew up in the 1970s, came of age in the 1980s, and have been a husband and father for over a decade. Sometimes I am able to step out of the bounds of my perspective and articulate a universal truth, and other times I am limited by who I am and can only speak to what I know. I no doubt maintain undiscovered biases and privileges, and I may not even know when these instances are, though I am committed to dismantling them whenever they crop up. I have made every attempt to consider feedback from people of different backgrounds and identities as I developed my teachings for tracking wonder, but I know that I can never speak for everyone. I write with humility, and I invite you to read with an unbiased openness so that wonder can work its magic through these words.

In interviews and conversations, people sometimes ask, "Shouldn't we just leave wonder alone?" and "Can you really teach something as spontaneous as wonder? Isn't that something that just comes with surprise or inspiration?" These questions might stem from a belief that something as truly exquisite and beautiful as the experience of wonder should not be reduced to pragmatism. I get that. I don't want to pin down wonder in my butterfly collection as a specimen of the human experience. If anything, over the past ten-plus years, I have aspired to unravel my assumptions about wonder and have explored well beyond my subjective experience, but at some point, one must be willing to make the case for what one believes so that many people can benefit.

My studies of Western wisdom traditions, philosophical herme-neutics, Eastern wisdom traditions, Native American stories, mythology and storytelling, creativity, entrepreneurship, and es-pecially psychology and neuroscience have influenced my study of wonder, as has my direct and immediate experience in the world. My intellectual and empirical journey has guided me toward cer-tain truths. One is this: wonder is a portal of consciousness that lets us see again what is beautiful and real, true and possible.

Every single one of us has this truly extraordinary capacity for wonder. Why *not* foster it in ways that help us individually and collectively contribute to the world in a positive way?

My work has led me especially to test these ideas among ev-eryday geniuses of creativity. They are the people who teach *me* what is possible. They are the entrepreneurs and executives, teachers and makers, parents and caretakers who have "out there" ideas and find ways to bring those ideas from fantasy to fruition. Sometimes they do so at great odds, without the ready resources of the rich and famous. Maybe they have young children or aging parents or a middle-aged brain or a full-time job. Inevitably, un-bidden surprises and obstacles could ambush their best-laid plans. What fascinates me about them is less their outward successes and more how they fashion lives of meaning and mastery along the way. More than any scholar, scientist, or obscure text, my cli-ents, students, participants, audiences, and community members have taught me the most about wonder and its very real appli-cations. These people are my heroes. This book puts their stories next to some of the more renowned geniuses of the world. This book is for them as it is for you.

In my consultancy and community, I hear people hungering for something beyond what they can attain with money. They don't just want to get a promotion, move into a bigger house, or take more expensive vacations. They don't want to hack time just so they can work more. This book is written specifically for people who want to feel alive in pursuit of ideas and activities that mean something to them at their core. They might desire to work through problems—big and small, personal and public—in novel and useful ways. It's also written for those people who want to contribute to something that makes other people's lives richer or better. Along the way, they want to navigate—not escape—disappointments and persistent challenges with more wit, flexibility, and fortitude. And they want to experience life's mysteries with wide-eyed openness and appreciation. Wonder, it turns out, is at the heart of these desires. If this describes you, read on.

When we bring wonder to the forefront of our daily, business, and creative endeavors, it makes our fullest expression of creativity possible. It also enables fruitful connections. It is time for our culture to evolve beyond an ideal of productivity that foregrounds control, efficiency, and discipline while ignoring what truly motivates us. Making this transformation requires that we develop a new set of skills and modes of perception, grounded in the infinite possibility of the present moment. This is Tracking Wonder.

CHAPTER 1

FLAMES

I PEELED A PAPERBACK edition of psychology's founding figure William James's *Essays on Psychology* from the burnt, blackened wall of my study. The book—the one that included the early American psychologist's prescient observations on different kinds of focus, on the need for relaxation, and on different states of consciousness—had been compressed into the wall from the pressurized fountain of the firefighters' hoses. I ripped from my singed walnut desk a copy of the Buddhist psychologist Mark Epstein's book *Going to Pieces Without Falling Apart* as I tried to hold it together. In a bit of a stupor, I scanned the room and took in the soaked books strewn on the hardwoods, a heap of ash where my modest meditation table had been, and dim rays of sunlight coming in through the holes the firefighters had knocked in the walls so the flames could escape.

It hadn't been an easy summer. My wife, Hillary, and I were newly married. A year before our wedding, we'd bought an 1850 farmhouse in New York's Hudson Valley. "The House of Great Strength," we called it. I—the wide-eyed dreamer, writer, and entrepreneur—had my sunny study that looked through a wide window onto my version of Walden Pond. Hillary—the acupuncturist, professor of Chinese Medicine, and business owner—relished her home office and sunny garden. We were ready at last to build our lives, our mutual businesses, and maybe someday a family. My parents divorced when I was thirteen, and as a teenager growing up with my bachelor father, I was on my own a lot—shopping for my own groceries, caring for the house, doing the laundry, and getting to school. Hillary and I each had had fleeting first marriages, and since we both savor prolonged solitude and quiet, neither of us were certain if we'd ever find a partner we could live with for several years. This was the first stable relationship and the first stable home we both had ever had. The morning that we moved in, we sat out back, gazing upon the large pond fed by a mountain stream. I said, "I think I could die here." We felt at home.

But that first summer, Hillary had two miscarriages. Our plans for children postponed, we weren't sure if we'd ever have the family we both deeply wanted. While I was leading a retreat not far from where we lived, I got what I thought was a spider bite. It grew black and red, and the night I came home I had fevers and cold sweats all night. The doctor saw a bull's-eye around the bite and quickly made the diagnosis of Lyme disease. The brutal antibiotics used to treat it slammed me on my back, leaving me exhausted and brain-fogged.

Then, on a July afternoon, Hillary and I had set out for a self-guided local farm tour in the hamlet where we live. By the time we left the first farm, an eerie, purple-colored storm had rolled in without warning. We pulled over and gawked at the lightning bolts that laddered from the sky to the earth. By the time the downpour sent us back home, four red trucks' worth of firefighters were pointing hoses toward our farmhouse. Lightning, the fire investigator later explained, had likely hit a black walnut tree that stands outside my study. The voltage apparently traveled under my floor, found a faulty electric wire that extends to the attic above my study, and fused the wire.

Flames roared through the room, burning twenty years of paper archives, destroying three hundred volumes of books, and melting my laptop that contained all the files of a new endeavor. This fire came way before the digital cloud, and I would never recover most of my work. Firefighters arrived, waterlogging what remained. After the smoke subsided, we were out of our home for nearly a year and a half. And within ten months, bitten by another tick, I was confirmed to have Lyme disease. Getting through the day with all my symptoms felt like trying to drive seventy miles per hour in second gear.

You likely have had your own version of house fires and tick bites—perhaps much more dire than this account—and if you have, I am truly sorry. We each construct a home of beliefs and values, relationships and work that makes up our reality. When the one you've made burns, how do you respond? How do you navigate these times when you're just starting a new dream or in the middle of one? Is the highest aim merely to get through the day as unscathed as possible? If you view life as a quest, as I do, then you acknowledge that challenges are part and parcel of what to expect on this path you've chosen. But, whoa!—and woe!—when those challenges are relentless, accumulative, and seemingly personal.

> **We each construct a home of beliefs and values, relationships and work that makes up our reality. When the one you've made burns, how do you respond?**

When I returned to our property to assess the damage, the sky showed through holes knocked out of the study's walls and ceiling. I am not one to give in easily to self-pity, but I really did start to question how it could be that once we had finally launched our dream, it could all vaporize in a flash of lightning. I wanted to cry, but I couldn't find the tears. I wanted to scream, but I couldn't direct the rage. Instead, I calmly gathered William James and Mark Epstein, bell hooks and Henry David Thoreau, and a score of poets, trying to build a familiar alliance of soul, music, and inner fire. I knew I had to muster every ounce of soldierly grit to persist, but I stood before that charred wall dizzy with both a load of anger and a shred of acceptance about what was to come next. I can only describe this mixed state as confusion, if not vertigo. I felt an uncomfortable urge to shut down.

Yet amid the black rubble, a small fluttering of yellow appeared. A monarch butterfly—likely showing up in an uncanny color morph—had slipped in and landed on a smoked-out shelf. Its fuzzy torso was the size of a baby's finger. It carried two enormous paragliding wings, etched like stained glass panels. They waved back and forth, back and forth, back and forth, like two palms pulsing in prayer.

For a moment, the pieces I was fiercely holding together inside me dissolved. For a moment, a strange sense of opening swept through me, wide and free. For a moment, among the ruins of our simple dreams, there fluttered a small, winged hope. Feeling that beauty and recognition, fleeting as it was, I knew ultimately we would be okay, maybe someday even better.

In the ensuing months, that monarch's surprising effect would remind me of what I had been pursuing before the fire: tracking wonder. I had been attuned to ordinary magic since I was a boy and into adulthood. In my earliest memory at four years old, I awoke in the middle of the night to see three smiling sea tortoises waltzing over my bed. That surreal moment lingered with me into my youthful forays. I yearned to discover such magical surprises in the everyday world, whether wandering through the woods or a book. At age eleven, I banged out adventure stories on my father's typewriter, with my neighborhood friends and me as characters. But by sixteen, I feared my imagination and capacity to experience the world through metaphors was slipping away. Yet in college I pursued writing poetry as a way to open my eyes again and express delight at the small things of the world. Writing and teaching as a young adult seemed to be the best ways to hold on to that dream space. But it was in my thirties while researching the imagination for another project that I found a name for what I had been seeking most of my life.

Before I met Hillary, I had traveled to the South Indian city of Chennai to study yoga with my teacher, Sri T. K. V. Desikachar. Desikachar's down-to-earth approach as well as yoga's flow of postures and breathing practices had unwound my tight body, unraveled my heart, and cleared my overwrought mind, but it had also reignited my imagination. Thanks to Desikachar, I discovered a text called the *Siva Sutras: The Yoga of Supreme Identity*. In a few commentaries, the scholar Jaideva Singh references a central passage that says, in essence, that the yogi who is able to experience the unity of consciousness throughout states of wakefulness, dreaming, and sleeping also experiences wonder, a joy-filled amazement at life.

Another kind of recognition struck me. That space where the waking world meets dreaming and wonder—that space has tantalized my imagination since I was a towheaded boy climbing trees and recording dreams. I read the passages again, relieved that this sage was advising me that I didn't have to renounce the world to attain fulfillment. The aspiration he described was to experience the delight of being, in all its peace and fire, right here. The drive to experience wonder, I realized, is what led me to all my areas of study and eventually to my professional teaching and consulting. "That's what I've always been seeking," I thought.

Adversity and uncertainty can spur a crisis of identity and of creativity. In such confusion, with little view of the future, you can slip into despair. You can feel as if you're dropping down that rabbit hole with no control. "Who are you?" the caterpillar asks Alice in Wonderland, and she doesn't know. From that dark and low place, your creativity seems shattered, just at a time when you need hope and openness to create something new. After my house burned, I could have remained in that hole. But wonder showed me a way out. Wonder lets us receive the uncertainty rather than flee to the next easy answer.

By the time of the fire, I had already scoured the journals, interviews, memoirs, and biographies of other writers, innovators, scientists, and artists to corroborate this feeling so many of us share but have difficulty articulating. It was a project of its own unwieldy nature, not yet explicitly connected to my career as an entrepreneur, consultant, and teacher. I had identified the state of wonder as the inspiration for the philosophy that gave rise to the Siva Sutras as well as to the first section of the Tao Te Ching. I had traced the concept in the mythologist Joseph Campbell's descriptions of the hero's journey. I had tracked the centuries-long debates about wonder among Christian theologians and Western scientists and philosophers.

I had tried to find explanations of my findings in the fields of psychology and neuroscience—although the literature was scarce at the time. I used my vacation time to pursue certain threads. Hillary and I once ventured to the Rio Grande border to spend a few days among North America's largest collection of cave rock art. With the guidance of Carolyn Boyd, an artist, archaeologist, and founder of the Shumla Archaeological Research and Education Center, we took a boat down the Pecos River. We encountered sophisticated images inscribed on stone by the people of the Lower Pecos Canyonlands over four thousand years ago. Boyd calls these sites North America's "oldest known books." I had another entry for my personal encyclopedia of wonder.

But then came the summer of lightning and fire that brought urgency to my wonder quest. Shortly after the yellow monarch alighted from the burnt, black wall, I realized that it had launched my true practice of tracking wonder. I knew I would only recover from all these setbacks if I learned how to harness wonder's force for my creative endeavors—right here, right now in this extraordinarily ordinary world. I couldn't let the butterfly become a beautiful fleeting moment. I needed it to be the first notes in a new symphony I would compose.

When Hillary and I finally moved back to the farmhouse, we also remodeled a room for our three-month-old baby girl. It seemed like no small miracle that this human being came to us amid such hardship. One crisp morning, I took our baby, Dahlia, for a walk down the road. Her tiny body snuggled into a swaddle strapped to my shoulders, she took in the crimson and golden leaves around us. I walked slowly, still affected by Lyme. Just as I felt a surge of fear that I might never be the larger-than-life papa I had at last imagined I could become, I paused.

I gazed into my infant girl's sky-blue eyes. I recognized in her gaze what I had been tracking since my boyhood—a natural capacity to see what is real and true, what is beautiful and possible without the filtered prejudices and judgments of adulthood. I made two silent vows. First, I promised to relearn from her the art of not-knowing. I also pledged to live a life so rich with creativity and wonder that she would embrace becoming a grown-up, too, instead of desperately clinging to her childhood.

I now have a more fully realized appreciation for wonder, and regularly open my Wonder Eyes. Doing so has guided me through many passages in life. I welcomed our equally miraculous second daughter four years after our first, helped build Hillary's business, recovered from Lyme, and developed Tracking Wonder into a dynamic consultancy and international community. Getting to the other side of trying times made me want to explore this question: *How could you practice fostering experiences of wonder in times of adversity and challenge?* My project of tracking wonder took on greater urgency as I deliberately tested out how to guide professionals, entrepreneurs, and others to harness their experiences of wonder. After testing out some new practices in training workshops, I witnessed wonder's magic on a diverse set of individuals. One insight especially stood out: *You can captivate, elevate, and enchant others. You can gift wonder.*

As I built the Tracking Wonder business, I devoted even more attention to tracking my personal practices at home and work, but I also continued to assimilate the emerging scientific studies on resilience, emotions, creativity, and innovation. I have interviewed and worked with people in many fields to get insight on other questions:

How do creative people thrive and keep open to possibility in times of challenge and change?

How do people advance their best ideas for a better world—without working themselves into the ground?

How do they keep pursuing a creative life of meaning and deep connection over several years?

It's no surprise that wonder keeps appearing in their lives.

FIVE INSIGHTS ABOUT WONDER

There are five other insights about wonder central to this book.

1. Wonder Is Fleeting Yet Enduring in Its Effects

An experience of wonder can happen like a flash of lightning or a fluttering of a butterfly, but it can have long-lasting effects. Most of our daily awareness is set unconsciously on a default mode of getting things done. We see each other and our work through biased filters. The more we experience, the thicker those filters can become. For a few seconds or minutes, an experience of wonder can dissolve those filters. We can see ourselves, others, our work, and the world around us in startling, even disorienting ways that are nonetheless real, true, and beautiful. Those few seconds or minutes experienced more often can gradually shift our general outlook and capacity to make things happen and make our lives extraordinary.

> **For a few seconds or minutes, an experience of wonder can dissolve those filters. We can see ourselves, others, our work, and the world around us in startling, even disorienting ways that are nonetheless real, true, and beautiful.**

2. Wonder Begins with an Infant's Eyes and Evolves to Adult Perception

My baby girl's eyes looked up at me searchingly. From our first breaths, wonder is initially visual, brought to us through our eyes.

If we can imagine wonder in part as a practice to regain this child-like visual perception, we can actively disrupt our eyes' default overfamiliarization with our physical world. As we age, our brains naturally categorize things, which helps us adapt to our environment but also leads to narrowed perception. As our weary eyes become Wonder Eyes again, we can appreciate the simple forms, shapes, and designs of things. When our perception widens, we can see new possibilities.

3. Wonder and a Creative Life Are Partners

In fact, recent developments in psychology corroborate that wonder fuels creative living. Wonder is the singular experience that resets our outlook outward to what is possible and expands our perspective. When we actively foster wonder daily, we are less likely to compartmentalize wonder to "creative pursuits," apart from the rest of life's "drudgeries." We bring more openness and curiosity to whatever challenges may arise—from finessing a four-year-old's temper tantrum to fulfilling a client deliverable to holding a team meeting to advancing your dream. We lead a creative life with less inner battle and with more integration.

4. Wonder Is Not Child's Play

A range of environmentalists, biologists, and theologians have called for a renewed sense of wonder to help us grown-ups learn how to live more openly and optimally in relation to one another as well as with the earth and all living beings. If we are going to advance our best ideas for a better world, then tracking wonder assumes a new height of responsibility. To put it simply, what we wonder at, we are more likely to care for. I want you to care about your best ideas to bring forth the best possible world. This book humbly invites you to do so.

5. Tracking Wonder Is a Skill and Mindset We Can Learn and Practice

Wonder, I have discovered, can be fostered and invited to accompany us as we endeavor to live, relate, and create fully in this complex world. We can track our own cognition and experiences and thus more readily appreciate and even extend these moments of wonder. The chapters that follow provide methods for developing these skills.

YOUR TRACKING WONDER JOURNEY

You cannot defer your own wisdom to the author of this book. It's essential that you go out and test things for yourself. This book's purpose is not only to offer a new understanding of wonder but also to help you trust your own experiences of wonder in your own full life.

Within each chapter you will find sections titled "Tracking Wonder Journey." These are invitations to reflect, assimilate, and test out one or more of the frameworks or principles presented. I suggest you keep all your tracking wonder exercises in one "Tracking Wonder" notebook. I recommend notebooks with dot-grid pages because they allow you to follow the form of expression wonder calls you to—whether you write, sketch, or doodle.

SNOW

While writing part of this book, my firstborn daughter was nine years old. It's a time when most children's brains develop in such a way that they grow ever more emotionally complex, develop more awareness of their own thoughts, and become more attuned to what other people think of them. She's given to a range of complex emotions like any healthy human being. She manages to spend many of her free hours absorbed in her own creation: writing and crafting her own storybooks from paper and yarn, sewing pillows for friends, knitting tiny clothes for her younger sister's stuffed animals, and composing quirky songs. One winter morning she had a snow day at home. I was in my study writing when she peeked in to ask what I was doing.

"I'm writing about this idea I have about young geniuses."

"Oh, that's me," she said with a smile.

"Ha. That's right"

"Papa, do you want to come out and play in the snow?"

"Oh," I said, "that sounds great, but I'm in the flow here and I don't want to interrupt it. Maybe later."

"Okay," she said, nonplussed, and off she went on her own adventures.

The room was quiet again, but of course now my mind wasn't. I typed a few more sentences, but Dahlia's invitation lingered. Outside the study window, snowflakes fell and started to cover the boughs as if miniature clouds had come down to roost. It would likely be this winter's last snow. I stared again at the screen and the blinking cursor.

Who was I kidding? I had a vow to keep.

CHAPTER 2

BIASES AGAINST WONDER

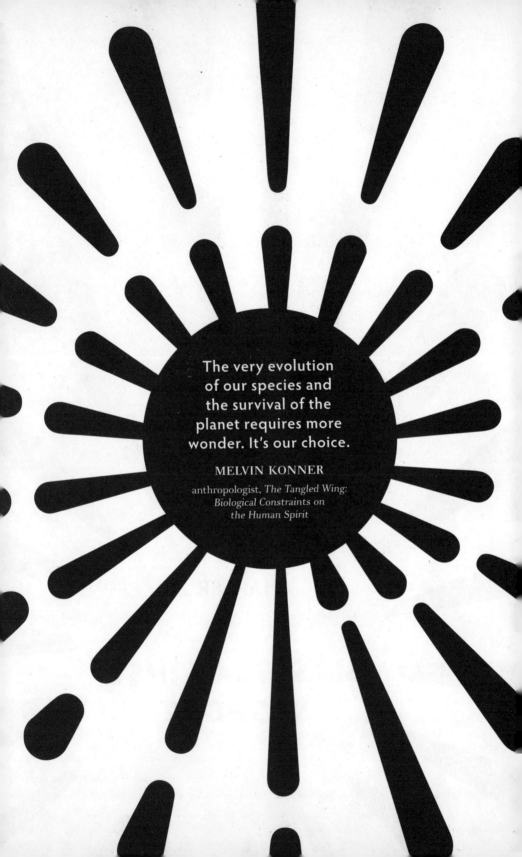

The very evolution
of our species and
the survival of the
planet requires more
wonder. It's our choice.

MELVIN KONNER

anthropologist, *The Tangled Wing:
Biological Constraints on
the Human Spirit*

A NEW STORY OF WHO WE ARE

A FEW DECADES AGO, the evolutionary biologist Harold Bauer encountered a chimp that captured his curiosity. Bauer was conducting research on chimpanzee social behavior in Tanzania's Gombe Stream Game Reserve, the same place where the audacious primatologist Jane Goodall established that chimpanzees make tools like human beings and share social behaviors similar to us. During Bauer's research, he noticed that one mature male would traipse through the lush forest, far off the trail for foraging food, until he would stop to gawk at a twenty-five-foot cascading waterfall. Imagine this spectacular sight: the hiss and roar, the buoyant misted sunlight amid the verdure of the tropical rain forest. Bauer reported that the chimp would simply sit and gaze as if enchanted. And then he'd lean in closer to the falls, dart back, rock, and pound his fists on the trees. The next day he'd return and repeat. Sit, gaze, rock, hoot. And the next day, and the next. A few other chimps followed suit. Why? From the point of view of an evolutionary biologist, who seeks behavioral explanations based on survival or reproduction, this activity seemed anomalous. The waterfall didn't serve as a key source of drinking water, and the chimps didn't have to cross this fall on their daily routes for foraging. In fact, the location was out of the way for pure survival needs. What was the evolutionary advantage?

Sure, we might regard this gazing, exclaiming chimp's behavior as quaint or cute, but maybe there's another story. The renowned biologist and anthropologist Melvin Konner suggests this as an explanation: Possibly one of our human ancestors some five million years ago came upon a waterfall or a wide ocean horizon and had a similar irresistible urge to stop and gawk. In such a response likely might have been what Konner describes as "the dawn of awe, of sacred attentiveness, of wonder." And yet, as Konner notes, every human infant begins life in a state of wide-eyed wonder. Their eyes function more optimally at this early stage compared to their other functions. They have a finely tuned apparatus for detecting novelty, gazing, and remaining attentive. Yet Konner laments that we are losing the sense of wonder, which he calls "the central feature of the human spirit." Konner believes that our species' evolution "requires more wonder. It's our choice."

How do we choose to make wonder central to our human experience again?

I want to pause here for a moment. I relish this story because of what it shows us about who we are at our core. Even though emotions such as fear, anger, and desire seem all-powerful when we are in their throes, I'd like to make the case for the primacy of wonder. In 1649, the philosopher René Descartes posited, as noted earlier, that "wonder is the first of all the passions," in a way prescient to what Konner observed about how infants spend their time. In fact, recent research supports a similar view of what motivates us. Our fundamental nature may not be to compete against but to cooperate with, empathize with, and be friendly to one another. Evolutionary anthropologists increasingly agree that our ancestors' earliest social skills evolved because natural selection favored cooperative social behaviors rather than aggression. This point of view makes sense. Consider the fact that for the vast majority of human existence, our ancestors lived in cooperative social bands that had to work together successfully to find food and raise families. Our hypercompetitive achievement-at-all-cost culture is something that we built; it wasn't how we began. With new, compelling evidence of our more open nature, we are scripting a fresh narrative of what qualities help us human beings not just survive but also thrive and flourish. Wonder also is a key player in that new narrative.

We are wired for wonder just like that waterfall-gazing chimpanzee, yet the world we've constructed often doesn't invite it. Oddly enough, in many ways the world conditions us against wonder.

THE BIAS AGAINST WONDER

To track wonder well, it helps to realize what you're up against in doing so.

Consider that we value productivity, and yet wonder does not appear productive. If you feel pressure to be more productive than creative at work, you're like eight in ten people surveyed by Adobe, the creative software company, in their 2012 *State of Create* study. The survey conducted among five thousand people across four countries reflected how our workplace culture favors hyper-productivity over creativity. In another annual study on Americans' vacation habits, millennials—contrary to the loafing, nomadic stereotype of their generation—want to be seen as "work martyrs" by their bosses. More so than older generations surveyed, they felt driven to overwork, to prioritize work at all costs instead of taking vacation days, and, at the very least, be perceived as irreplaceable.

The Atlantic's Derek Thompson has gone so far as to claim that these days, even young, rich, college-educated Americans are worshipping work like a religion in a way he has termed "Workism: the belief that work is not only necessary to economic production, but also the centerpiece of one's identity and life's purpose."

But, we must wonder, at what cost?

THE SURPRISING GIFT IN THE BREAK

Many of us have unconsciously accepted a bias for constant productivity and a prejudice against wonder. This bias might account for why people in some cultures influenced by a Protestant work ethic once equated wonder with an illness called "the wonders." I often imagine that during the Industrial Revolution many farmers and workers in Scotland and Ireland might have viewed anyone who wondered at anything for too long as a dreamy, foolish time-waster. Imagine a boy caught up in his own inventions, drawings, or daydreams. He might've been tagged, derisively, by locals as "'ater his 'oonderments" (after his wonderments). Never mind that that dreamy boy might become a scientist or inventor whose wondering might lead to improved working conditions. In short, if you wondered, you weren't being productive. "No time for a break!" a real or imagined supervisor might say. "Get back to work!"

Wonder might stun you into utter inaction, but is such a state an illness? The Cornish, Devon, and Welsh languages also have variations of the word *wonders* related to numbness, cold-induced tingling in the fingers and toes, and weakness. People who suffer from hypothermia might describe an almost pleasurable stupor of gazing and no-thinking—not unlike the gawking chimp. The condition puts us in a nonbustling, nonanalytical, receptive state. It often widens the pupils and throws our mouths agape.

But unlike other strong emotions, wonder does not make us want either to react or flee. When we watch the wind ripple hypnotically across pond water, our bodies and brains don't register strong attraction signals to grab the waves. We simply receive the object of our astonishment without feeling compelled to manipulate it. In our hustle-and-distract workaday world, wonder is the lunch break that rarely happens.

So some of us have generations of accumulated cultural debris, so to speak, to clear as we track wonder. Consider a lighthearted character from my kids' favorite bedtime story who embodies the hidden treasure of wonder. Meet Frederick the field mouse. One autumn, his family scurries about to dig out their burrow and gather as many nuts as they can to tide them over for the winter season. Yet Frederick chooses to rest in a corner. The other mice ask him repeatedly, What is he *doing*? Not much. Frederick essentially daydreams. By all appearances, he has a case of "the wonders"—or in Melvin Konner's words, he chooses wonder.

As the days grow darker and colder, and the nuts are in short supply, the other mice start to shiver and whine. But then Frederick stands, clears his throat, and recites what he in fact has been "storing up" in his imagination: poetry. His words of sunlight brighten their dark days. His images of color enhance the gray. The other mice beam as they feel warm and alive inside, wholly grateful for Frederick's wondrous work. My girls savor hearing this charming and surprising story penned by Leo Lionni, and I appreciate that they are learning at this age that while we need industry to survive and contribute, we also must choose wonder in order to thrive and create.

Like the chimp, like Frederick, like my infant girl on that autumn day, wonder arrests our eyes from always hunting. We pause and take our break and let our senses receive part of the world's surprising beauty. This receptive quality distinguishes wonder from other emotions. If we feel love or infatuation for someone, by contrast, we're magnetized to that person, we contact the person (repeatedly), or we try to see them again. If, on the other hand, we experience fear of giving a speech, we might avoid the work and spend a day rearranging our books rather than developing and rehearsing the talk. Love attracts; fear repels. Wonder, however, pauses us in openness.

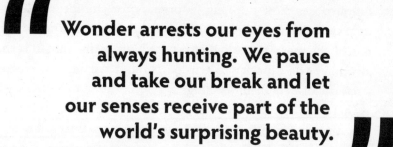

> **Wonder arrests our eyes from always hunting. We pause and take our break and let our senses receive part of the world's surprising beauty.**

After a couple of centuries of constant bustle and building that has brought with it world wars, diseases of all kinds, social isolation, and rampant inequality, maybe it behooves us to be less dismissive of such receptive, open qualities. Wonder could be the hero who rescues us from a cubicle or prison of our own making.

CURE YOUR DOWNERS WITH A CASE OF THE WONDERS

Our practice in tracking wonder begins, though, not with trying to change the world but in disrupting our mind's default settings. Even when we're not consciously doing or thinking anything, sections of our brain still produce a steady stream of cognitive activity. There's a name for these brain regions that light up when this near-unconscious thinking is active: the default mode network (DMN). Although the DMN can be a rich source of creative insight, if left unchecked, these "default" thought patterns can keep you in an agitated, glum, or worried state throughout much of your days.

We each have these default settings. They're normal and pop up when you're not intentionally directing your attention toward a specific task. These cognitive patterns often go unchecked. But default story-making and self-sabotage do not have to be your daily reality. I call them out so you can start to detect them.

You may have acute patterns of fret and regret that hum in the background of your conscious mind like irritating flies. We human beings have funny wiring, and this default wiring can serve its purposes. Fret can help us prepare for the future. Regret can help us make meaning of the past and try better next time. But one of the many remarkable things about being human is that we also have the capacity to trip our brain's wiring and create new patterns of default processing.

There is a simple way to begin tracking default patterns so you can disrupt them. Let's call them downer patterns. Remarkably, an anagram of the word *wonder* is *downer*. As a lover of wordplay, I never take these kinds of coincidences in letter form too lightly or too seriously. So, imagine that the word *wonder* got itself in a deep gutter. *Gutter* is the term for the inner margin of adjacent inner margins of facing pages when a book is open. No matter how hard it tried, *wonder* couldn't get itself out of this gutter. Its letters got jumbled from the struggle, and it became so disheartened that it literally turned into *downer*. Well, when we're in our own gutters—whether that's emotional discomfort, hunger, stress, fatigue, you name it—we also become downers.

Our downer mind, as opposed to our wonder mind, sabotages our best intentions. Let's say you send a friend a time-sensitive email, and after a day you get no response. Your downer mind might conjure a story about how the friend has a problem with you and so is ignoring you. Or let's say that you're working on an important presentation to a new audience, but voices from your downer mind raise all kinds of false stories about your lame abilities or low intelligence. Usually your downer stories simply are not true, and they're rarely worth obsessing over.

These downer patterns often arise in three forms—your own self-regard, your situation, and your ideas (your projects or endeavors). For instance, a downer pattern might sound like, "I am not any good. I am a failure. I don't have the X [the talent, gumption, intelligence, charm] to advance my ideas, reach my goals, or enjoy life." A situation might be the consequences of your life situation or your work-from-home situation. A situation downer pattern might sound like, "This situation is wrecking my life. It has destroyed any opportunities I had." A downer pattern related to your ideas themselves might sound something like, "My projects are not as important as other urgent matters. My ideas are not worth the investment in time, energy, and resources." Do these patterns sound familiar? Of course they do. You have a beautiful human mind worth tracking.

One of the quickest ways to disrupt the default downers is to stop, look, and listen. I take walks down our country road several times a week. It's astounding to me still that among the rows of evergreens, streams, and wildflower meadows there are also regular roadside appearances of beer cans, wrappers, and plastic bags. My default downer mind goes into annoyance, if not anger, when I see this litter. Before our firstborn came along, I wanted to write letters to the editor and meet with the town supervisor to do more than the annual Earth Day cleanups. But then I started walking our firstborn girl, Dahlia, down the same road, and by the time she was five, she decided she wanted to push the stroller with us and pick up the trash. So we put on gloves and gathered the litter. Doing so actually forced me to look at the litter. It made me more curious about and less judgmental of our neighbors. Once I found a stash of receipts that I waded through not to be nosy but to wonder what my neighbors' lives were like. They bought a lot of office supplies and food. Just like us. Once we even found not far from our house a woman's red vinyl high-heeled shoe. Just one. What was the story behind that?

I've also trained employees and teams to pause and gaze in the middle of their days. We call these breaks "wonder interventions at work." This particular wonder intervention is called

Pause-Gaze-Praise. The idea is that when you are working and you notice your temples tightening, your eyesight narrowing, your body aching, and your mind spinning downward, you train yourself to pause. The employees and teams each learn to look away from what they're busily doing—especially if they've been staring for hours at a screen—and instead gaze upon something ordinary right around them. A chair or paper clip suffice. They learn to let their eyes soften and simply receive the shape, hue, and design of the thing itself without *thinking* about the thing. Then they take a moment to appreciate what they gaze upon. They might note simple words of praise in their mind or on a notepad. They learn to open their Wonder Eyes for just a moment. They learn not only to work well but also to break better. They learn to choose wonder.

If this wonder intervention sounds a little goofy to you, consider Mike Ilardo. Mike is VP at a growing manufacturer of wireless site components. He's also the father of two young sons and husband to a very considerate wife. I met Mike on the first day of a multiday Tracking Wonder immersion I led at a venue in Santa Cruz, California. When I asked him what brought him to the immersion, he said, "My wife sent me here as a birthday present. To *her*." For over nineteen years, Mike has worked hard at his position to secure a living for his family. At first the job was fun, but as the company grew, so did his responsibilities and problems. As problems grew, his vision shrank. His wife sent him to this immersion perhaps to bring back his passion for life. Throughout the next few days at the immersion, Mike began to reclaim his young genius qualities, and his eyes began to open. When I asked him two weeks after the event what stuck with him the most, he wrote this:

" For me, the moment when things really began to click was following the Pause-Gaze-Praise exercise that we did outside. I think that helped me to realize that I need to take the time from the hustle and bustle of everyday life to enjoy what is right in front of me. It's a great way to reset when I get stuck in the default closed mind. It made me think about what is really important to me, and that I need to take more time to acknowledge those things. Since I have been back home and at work, I have noticed that I have been paying more attention to the people in my life and also my everyday surroundings. It was a real eye-opener. "

A year later he wrote to me that he was now appreciating working in his backyard more often and that in the cold of December he and his son were taking frequent dips in the Pacific Ocean—much to the surprise of bundled-up onlookers. His wife, Mike told me, was elated by the results of her birthday gift a year earlier.

UP YOUR RATIO OF DAILY WONDER

You're not going to live and create with wonder all day long. That would be as fatiguing and counterproductive as trying to be happy or compassionate all day long. For instance, all of us live at times in the neighborhood of worry. If you dwell there, maybe you have a short fuse or get anxious often. When someone or something poses a challenge to what you want, you close down and feel disconnected. Your days unravel with an endless list of meaningless to-dos. When you live here, you dwell more in default mode and your response to life forms default grooves. All of us visit this place, but none of us want to live here if we are to pursue a creative life of meaning and mastery.

At different times in my life, I've been awakened by an internal alarm clock at 3:00 or 4:00 a.m. With my wife sound asleep beside me, my mind scans darkness for its internal radio until it tunes into station WRRY. It plays my downer mind's top ten favorite hits. Hit number one: "You're No Good" (not a talented enough creative producer or an attentive enough business owner or a thoughtful enough team leader or a responsive enough consultant or a wise enough father). There is a central difference between caring and worrying. Caring—which wonder gives rise to in the facet of connection—aims toward other people or issues or meaningful endeavors greater than you. Worrying is often all about you. That me-centeredness gets in the way of your tending to your dreams with the openness and versatility they deserve.

The counterresponse to this me-centered attention is not to live perpetually in the neighborhood of wonder. Instead, the invitation here is to up the ratio of how often you can let wonder visit. You can experience your days and advance your dreams with a little less worry and a little more wonder.

FROM DOWNER TO WONDER

This invitation is to learn to track and disrupt your daily downer patterns. Have your Tracking Wonder notebook handy.

Identify Your Downer Patterns

Take a moment right now to recenter your attention within. Assume a posture of dignity and stability. Bring your attention to the rhythms of your breath. Allow the next inhalation to extend to four seconds. And out for four seconds. Again.

Now take a moment to be curious and nonjudgmental as you ask yourself, "What are one to two of my common downer patterns that block my ability to feel fulfilled or otherwise enjoy any moment?"

Does your downer mind often tell you a false story about your faults, limitations, or traits?

Does your downer mind often project a false narrative about your circumstances?

Does your downer mind scoff at your dreams or ideas?

Open your eyes and take out your Tracking Wonder notebook. In one sentence or a few words, describe a downer. Do so with openness and curiosity, and maybe poke a little fun at these patterns because, really, they're mostly the result of our mind's whacky activity. Your notebook in this way becomes a personal field guide of your perceptions. I encourage you to normalize, instead of pathologize, your cognitive patterns.

Break Better and Increase Your Wonder Ratio Throughout the Day

You might not measure wonder easily, but you can track it. For instance, contrast what a default day might look like versus a day where wonder intervenes for good measure.

Default Days	Moments to Invite Wonder
Perform your indoor morning routine in a rut.	Step outdoors for five minutes in the middle of your routine.
When someone interrupts your focus either while cooking or working, get irritated.	Pause. See the person. Ask a question.
Drive your commute on autopilot.	Challenge yourself to notice one thing you've never noticed before, or dare to take a detour.
Measure your day by how many to-dos you checked off.	Measure your day by noticing the sound of a crow or observing someone's eyes for the first time in years.
When you hit a creative wall, tell yourself, "This sucks. I'm no good."	When you hit a creative wall, pause. Look up and wonder how you could get over, around, under, or through it. Where there's wonder, there's a way.

Default Days	Moments to Invite Wonder
When you come home from hours of running errands or being at work, then drop your bags, pass by people with an automated "Hello" and collapse behind a computer or in front of a television and veg out.	When late afternoon comes and your focus grows tired, pause and take a walk "without why," or even better, a saunter. Open yourself to the many hidden gems in your neighborhood and your imagination's net.

You might make a similar chart in your notebook. On the left, write down your default actions in the morning, afternoon, and evening. On the right, give yourself an invitation to track wonder instead by disrupting the default pattern. Can you remind yourself to pause, gaze, and praise for only five minutes? Instead of getting irritated by noise, can you pause and imagine the noise as music? I know that's a stretch for some of us, but it is part of the practice.

Tomorrow, how can you up the wonder ratio and disrupt the default and the downer? Set an intention and plan ahead to invite wonder into your day. If you keep a planner, write down one way you can remember to disrupt a downer pattern or default habit from the workaday world. Some of my clients stick Wonder Post-its on their computer with notes like, "Look up today!" or "Take a wonder intervention today!"

Don't make tracking wonder another chore or to-do item. I can assure you that with this increased awareness, something will shift in your attention and how you experience your life.

So much is possible in the hours that compose one day. Even right now.

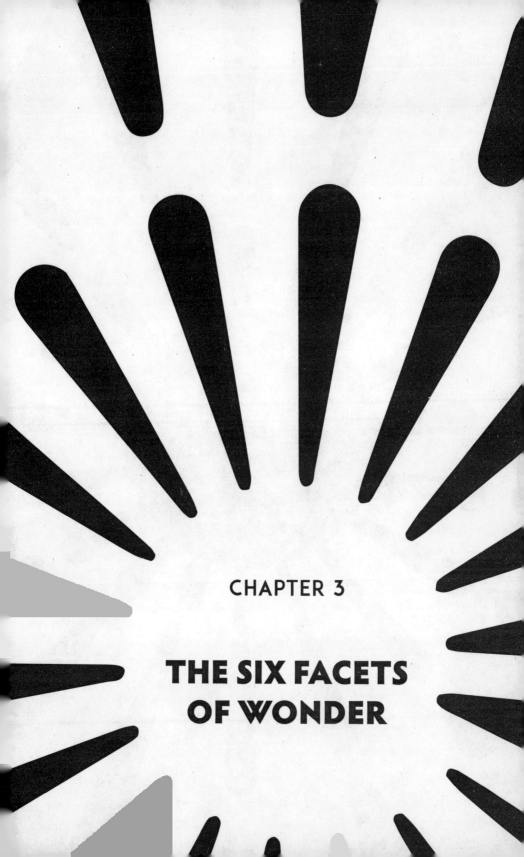

CHAPTER 3

THE SIX FACETS
OF WONDER

My experience is what
I agree to tend to.

WILLIAM JAMES

early founder of
American psychology

WHAT EXACTLY ARE WE TRACKING?

WONDER IS THE SINGULAR experience that, for a fleeting moment, disrupts our awareness and dissolves our biases so we may see again what is real and true, beautiful and possible. Wonder is essential for us to advance our best ideas for a better world. It also is our biological and neurological pause-and-reset button that makes us feel, like that hooting chimp, wildly alive again and ready to approach any challenge. Survival of the wondrous.

The question, then, is *how* do we track such experiences? As we'll discover in this chapter, to track wonder is both simple and complex. Why? Because wonder is pervasive and evasive. Wonder can arrive when you appreciate the beauty of stirring soup made from vegetables you and your neighbors have grown, or when a sunset viewed from your yard casts oranges and purples across cumulus clouds that engulf the sky like breathing beings—a splendor that unexpectedly prompts you to take charge of your life's next beautiful phase. The moments come and go in a flash, but their effects can linger if we heed them. Tracking wonder *is* a skill set you can build.

To help you understand when you are experiencing wonder, it helps to make subtle distinctions. First, let's be clear that I am not referring as much to wonder in its verb form. To wonder, the action, is more like questioning, but wonder is not curiosity. Curiosity propels us to investigate, to pick apart a clock's cogs and wires, whereas wonder surprises and delights, receives and conceives. Yet, as we'll see in later chapters, wonder often incites curiosity. Yes, wonder can incite wondering. Wonder is a heightened state of consciousness and emotion brought about by something unexpected. While it is a perceptual experience that happens in the mind, it can radiate through your body's parasympathetic nervous system, which is the opposite of the fight-or-flight response, helping you to relax and open to insight and possibility.

Second, some people associate joy with wonder, but they are not the same. I think of joy as wonder's more effusive cousin, because joy beams like sunshine, whereas wonder can dwell in that emotional space between sunlight and shadow. In this sense, wonder is not partial only to happiness and is no exclusive member of the Optimist's Club. It can be tinged with melancholy or sadness and still carry profound insight.

Third, wonder is unique as well because it often commingles with awe, which I think of as wonder's larger-than-life cousin. Awe arises in moments of vastness as we feel small while gazing at an infinitely starry sky, a tumultuous and vast ocean, or a towering and cavernous Gothic cathedral. Wonder, though, can appear in the size of an ant. More than awe, wonder helps us see the familiar in a fresh, new way. We can appreciate just how extraordinary an ordinary moment can be.

THE SIX FACETS OF WONDER

In my years of tracking wonder, I have discovered that it comes in different forms—or facets, as I prefer to call them. Think of facets as the faces on a prismatic gem that each catch the light and broadcast their own sparkly magic. Imagine for a moment a vast net that extends across the sky for as far as you can see and beyond. At each of the net's nodes is a radiant gem. Each gem contains many finely cut facets, and each facet reflects upon the facets of the other gems, creating an infinite interrelated tapestry of light. When you experience the facets of wonder, you might catch a glimpse, for instance, of how the tree outside your window reflects upon the grass and how the grass reflects upon the fence and how the fence reflects upon the sky and how the sky reflects upon you and how you reflect upon everything around you. It's all a net of reflected light.

This radiant display represents the Buddhist idea of Indra's Net, that everything in the cosmos is interrelated. I refer to it here to give you a sense of what experiencing wonder's facets can feel like.

Based on my research and work with people from different walks of life, I developed a vocabulary of the different facets of wonder to equip you to track wonder more confidently. Think of this vocabulary as similar to some forms of therapy in which you learn to identify and become more aware of emotions, such as anger or fear, so you can manage them better. In certain spiritual traditions, teachers also name states of awareness to help meditation practitioners navigate them more skillfully. Likewise, knowing the facets of wonder better equips you to be aware of these rippling moments and gradually foster more of these expansive experiences. Remember that by disrupting your default mode of perception and cognition, wonder provides a launchpad for creativity, resilience, and connection.

I've also given each facet a respective metaphor. The right metaphors communicate to us beyond rational language and help us more fully experience the essence of a facet.

OPENNESS, the wide-sky facet, is a wide-eyed wonder among us grown-ups. It is the capacity to perceive a subject or situation anew while pursuing new knowledge or launching and even executing an endeavor. If you hunger to taste more than vanilla, then tracking this facet can boost your creative approach to life and work. (I don't mean to disparage this delicate Polynesian flavor, which was quite exotic when first introduced to the Western world—and still brings me gustatory wonder in a thick milkshake.) When fear or self-doubt holds you back from pursuing a meaningful dream or endeavor, then this facet can be an important ally. Why? It is the talent of knowing when and how to suspend biases, to dare to un-know, and to be receptive to possibilities instead of immediately judging them. I also call this facet intelligent naiveté, the nuances of which we explore in chapter 4.

CURIOSITY, the rebel facet, is the proactive, playful, and creative mindset that comes out of wonder's more receptive nature. Curiosity lets us pursue discovery, honor the quirky things that interest us, and keep learning by doing so we live in more wondrous questions than definitive answers. With this mindset you learn to become more engaged with new experiences and actively seek novel perspectives and useful outcomes both to everyday problems and to your creative pursuits. Curiosity questions the "way we've always done things" and prompts you to take action on those questions.

BEWILDERMENT, the deep woods facet, is the disorienting facet of wonder. It is a response to simultaneous positive and negative input that could spark inaction or fear. When in bewildering confusion, you can feel at once exhilarated by the new world you could be venturing into and disoriented, if not lost. When you track this facet, you learn to fertilize confusion because you can take that restless energy of profound uncertainty as creative fuel to redefine your purpose and your evolving identity. Not knowing—who you are becoming, what to do next, or what will happen next—is a feeling most of us are uncomfortable with, but if you track bewilderment, you can ultimately reach creative and personal breakthroughs.

HOPE, the rainbow facet, is a buoyant feeling of possibility amid uncertainty that often illuminates the most profound changes in our lives. While we endure adversity or crisis, this facet of wonder momentarily points the way proactively toward a better future. Much richer than mere wishful thinking, hope can buoy you in turbulent times and help you find a way through suffering.

CONNECTION, the flock facet, is the facet that we feel when wonder allows us to be, create, and feel supported with others. In these times when many people report feeling lonely or isolated, this facet is crucial to our fulfillment because it teaches us how to attune with loved ones and deepen our working relationships. True connection also is a basic human need that contributes to our health and happiness. Practices of connection teach us that we are often better when we do it together, open up in the face of bias against others, and gather supportive packs around us to support our creative lives.

ADMIRATION, the mirror facet, builds on the other facets because it is an emotion focused on others, specifically those whose model of character or craft encourage us to become more of our genius selves. To admire someone is to feel wonder at a display of someone's excellence. While admiration's sneaky twin, envy, might also motivate us toward getting better at how we do what we do, it is tinged with negativity. We can track both admiration and benign envy. Tracking admiration as a facet of wonder reminds us how to see ourselves as sources of wonder for others. Ultimately, learning how to praise, appreciate, and create enchanting experiences for others is how you keep this mirror facet reflecting in multiple directions.

A note on which facets you might start tracking: These six facets can work optimally for you in pairs. Together, the facets of openness and curiosity tap your innate ability to live each day with a more creative, less reactive, mindset. These two facets are foundational, and in my experience with clients and students, they are perhaps the easiest among the six to begin tracking. Fostering the two facets of bewilderment and hope together can strengthen your resilience and fortitude in trying times. Because they can shift, if not transform, your view of the world or your life in beneficial ways, tracking these two facets can be profoundly rewarding. If you or someone you know is having hard times, start with these two. Together, when you track connection and admiration, you learn to shift your direction outward and deepen your relationships with others. This other-orientation makes them essential facets for our times.

The chapters ahead will explore these facets and give you the tools for recognizing, tracking, and integrating them into your way of life. Tracking wonder means that you choose to pay more attention to all these facets. With practice you will start to recognize them in certain moments, and my aim is that you will foster a sort of intimate relationship with these facets in a way that lets you appreciate this one life in all its glory and challenges even more.

WHAT WE MEAN BY "TRACK"

If you've ever tried to watch your thoughts while seated in meditation or attempted to consciously shift your mood from dour to energized, you have an idea of how challenging it can be to "track" your interior world. What exactly does that mean—to track? To track something, whether an emotion or animal, requires different faculties than our standard awareness. Just ask a master animal tracker. These experts know how to detect the signs of specific animal behavior—such as scat, prints, and chew marks—largely to help us understand how animal populations move, migrate, and evolve over time. They can examine the bend of grass, scratches on bark, and urine scent on rocks to follow a single animal's path for miles to eventually find the animal. And if they don't find the animal, these clues they have been accumulating add up to a story of where the animal came from and where it is going.

I spent a weekend with such a tracker. His story could give you a sense of what a daily adventure it can feel like to track wonder in this world. Mark Elbroch, the author of several animal tracking field guides, is a lead scientist for the global wild cat conservation organization Panthera. Elbroch has followed lions in the Sahara among the Kalahari native trackers, gotten intimate with bobcats in Yellowstone National Park, and in one startling instance was nearly stampeded by a fierce hippo.

As Elbroch relayed to me, once while camping in Los Padres National Forest in California, he headed out on the day's final tracking walk at dusk. He hoped to get one last glimpse of fox or maybe coyote prints before he settled into his campsite. He hiked toward a nearby sandy wash where prints register clearly, and in the fading light he crossed more than he had bargained for: big, fearsome cat prints. "Cougar," he said to himself. Male cougars, among the most powerful and wild of the United States' felines, can weigh as much as 150–200 pounds. Twenty-five miles from the nearest town with night coming on, Elbroch took a deep breath as his eyes and mind measured the distance between steps, and his imagination shaped the feline's size and gait. "Probably a female," he thought. "What's she doing here? How long ago was she on this path? What's her mood?"

He walked on and remembered what a veteran tracker in Africa told him when a leopard crept near their campfire one night: "You're allowed to be afraid if you find her tracks on top of yours." Two hours later, he circled around to his own tracks he had made beside the original cougar prints. The half-moon broke from the clouds and then he saw it. Hers were on top of his.

He wasn't tracking the cougar; the cougar was tracking him.

It was a long—and *brisk*—two-mile hike to his car where Elbroch slept. The next morning, he found the cougar's marks along his campfire's edge. He followed them for about ten meters off the trail and traced her tracks to where she had picked up two kittens and walked directly on top of his own boot tracks, up to his truck and campsite's borders, to the nearby spring for a drink, and back to his site. He could imagine her curiosity, and her hunger. He felt for a moment strangely, intimately connected.

One takeaway for us is that the faculties that real animal tracking demand surpass the analytical intellect. As Elbroch told me, a tracker is both a scientist and a storyteller. It requires imagination to envision a bear's shape and movement, empathy to sense a leopard's mood, and intuition to find where a coyote might set up its den. Above all else, a tracker must shift between knowing and not-knowing. "Stay open to possibilities," Elbroch implores his students. "Suspend what you think you know."

So it is with tracking wonder, too. So, how do we track wonder in this workaday world?

TRACK WONDER WITH A DOSE

You can be on the lookout for wonder in the most ordinary places that you might not have suspected. Begin with your heart. If emotionally attuned, you can start by noticing when you feel surprised and elevated by what you see or sense, or even by what someone says or does. Yet also pay attention to the less delightful experiences where wonder can appear. When you're navigating emotional storms of confusion, doubt, or grief, for instance, seek moments that can uplift you. One of my colleagues was grieving her mother's death with a small group of family by taking a memorial walk on a nature path. Suddenly, a red-shouldered hawk swooped down onto a stump, in clear view of my colleague's toddler daughter. As everyone watched, the hawk bobbed its head and displayed its wings, its eyes transfixed on the little girl. No one moved as they saw the little girl reach both her hands out toward the raptor. With a majestic flap of its wings, it soared off into the trees, taking a flight path in front of the family. "This hawk had us all transfixed," my colleague said. "We all were rapt with wonder, and also *wondering*, if the spirit of my mom was somehow at work and communicating with my young daughter. I'll never forget how that moment allowed us to see another wondrous side of our grief."

Notice wonder when you feel confused. As the psychologist Kelly Bulkeley says, "To feel wonder is to experience a sudden *de-centering* of the self." Such surprises of the soul can bring about deeper truths. If you're a seeker who lives with more questions than answers about life, purpose, and meaning, then chances are you have an idea of what I mean.

Notice wonder in your own mind, too. Especially if you're less of a feeler and more of a thinker, you might notice when your mind surprises you or when someone else's idea opens you up to new possibilities. Yes, your mind contains wonders—not just monkeys, as my Zen meditation teacher John Daido Loori used to say. If you've ever had one of those "shower moments" when, for instance, the way water gliding down the shower wall gives you fresh insight, you can appreciate that the very nature of your mind and its intricate workings can elicit wonder. No matter how much science I absorb, I still feel a bit unraveled at times that we human beings are here on this intricately structured planet, able to live and move and make, breath after breath—and we possess a consciousness and brain that lets us both recognize and appreciate this one life. Listen to scientists such as Carl Sagan or Neil deGrasse Tyson talk about the universe's vastness and you'll appreciate how wonder constantly fuels us to discover new galaxies out there and in here. In this way, wonder gives rise to the imagination as it fosters insights and enchants us with possibility.

You also can track your responses to art, performance, and natural beauty. For instance, pay more attention to how a musical performance or Olympic athlete's performance stuns you into mouth-gaping silence, or even a moment when you suddenly stop in your tracks to appreciate the intricate features of a beetle's armor or the labyrinthine wood-grain patterns of the floor beneath your feet. Finally—and perhaps especially important for our times—you also can experience wonder in the space between you and someone else. When you feel surprisingly bonded, even for a fleeting moment, either in conversation or collaboration or sexual intimacy, wonder appears.

The facets of wonder will help you track all these kinds of experiences.

I hope you are starting to appreciate the places where wonder might emerge—in a conversation, in a movie theater, in your musing mind, in the bedroom or boardroom, or in an existential quandary.

Perhaps you're still wondering where to start. Note that I resist codifying how we track wonder. To make too rigid of a method defies wonder's ephemeral beauty. Yet as a longtime teacher in different contexts, I feel compelled to offer you a tool as we begin this quest together. Especially if you feel like a beginner here, this mnemonic might help you take first steps. It's called DOSE.

THE **D** IS FOR DETECTING YOUR DEFAULT PATTERN OR DOWNER REACTION. You started this practice in the previous chapter. Notice when you're numbing out, tuning out, or dropping into a pattern of fret, regret, or unwanted distraction. Acknowledge if your mind, heart, or spirit feel closed in an undesired way.

THE **O** SIGNALS YOU TO OPEN UP, PAUSE, AND FEEL. Be curious about how your default pattern feels in your body. When you worry, do your temples hurt? Do your brows furrow? Does your vision seem narrow? How could this moment be different? How could you pause your mind's activity and open up to more possibility?

WITH OUR **S**, WE SEEK OUT WONDER. This book's stories and Tracking Wonder Journey trainings and exercises will inspire you to do just that, but you ultimately will create your own ways. And if wonder tracks you like the cougar tracked Elbroch, then that *S* also stands for surprise!

FINALLY, WITH THE **E** WE EXTEND THE WONDER. We reflect upon, make, and share our appreciation of the ripples of wonder.

Do you want a DOSE of wonder? Detect. Open up. Seek. Extend. It's a foundational practice to up your daily dosage of wonder.

Let's linger on that last part—*Extend*—for a moment. Remember wonder as the red fox of experiences. Now you see it, now you don't. As the prominent psychologist and early wonder researcher Jonathan Haidt said to me, "[Wonder] is nearly impossible to measure." To foster such nuanced and shape-shifting experiences requires less that we measure and pin it down with scientific precision and more that we learn to track and, well, at times be in wonder at wonder itself.

> **Experiences of wonder are often ephemeral in duration but can be everlasting in effect.**

Yet there is a crucial point here. Experiences of wonder are often ephemeral in duration but can be everlasting in effect. When a moment of wonder means something to you—whether it is a child saying your name for the first time or the luminescent way autumn sunlight dappled across the front lawn when you received some bad news—that moment lingers and ripples. Such a moment makes a deeper impression in a brain region where long-term memories are stored: the hippocampus. When the hippocampus's circuitry lights up, you often can recall the specific tenor of the toddler's voice or the way the autumn breeze brushed your cheek that day. We can make meaning from moments, however subtle or fleeting. There are three common ways I have led clients, students, and participants to make meaning in this final step of DOSE. It's that final E, which stands for *extend the wonder*, that often allows us to create a new neural pathway. Here's how you extend:

REFLECT. People who actively make meaning of their lives periodically pause and reflect upon their experiences. Your Tracking Wonder notebook will be a ready tool for such reflection where I encourage you to write, sketch, doodle, outline, or illustrate as a way to reflect upon and track your reflections.

MAKE. To make meaning, we human beings make things. Whether you make a photograph slideshow or album, write a poem or an article, or build a bench for your meditation garden, simple acts of making often are ways to elongate a moment that means something to us.

SHARE. Don't be embarrassed to tell somebody about the spectacular double rainbow that appeared over your neighbor's house on the very day you needed to see it, or to share with your friend how awestruck you were by a maple tree's leaves turned blood red. We could all get better practiced at sharing such moments of renewed perception, instead of the latest sensational headline that raises our ire.

Reflecting, making, and sharing all are active ways we help impressions of small moments get stored in the hippocampus, extending our wonder for longer than a few seconds.

Wonder is right here. Let's invite it out of its lair.

TAKE A WONDER INVENTORY

The following practices can help you pay more attention to small moments of wonder in your everyday life and actively increase your wonder ratio. In your Tracking Wonder notebook, explore responses to these three questions:

When Was a Time Within the Past Few Days or Weeks You Felt Surprisingly Expansive in Heart and Mind?

Maybe a scene from a film or a piece of music suddenly gave you the chills. If you like ideas, you might have experienced the wonder of thinking while reading or having a conversation or listening to a podcast. Maybe you actively disrupted a default downer pattern. For instance, when I get locked into a downer mindset during the day, I try to take a break and step outside for five minutes or take a "drive without why" for ten minutes. When did you recently have such a moment of surprising expansiveness?

In your Tracking Wonder notebook, list one or more of your own such experiences or moments, no matter how ordinary or extraordinary. What one small shift could you make to your daily rhythm to experience more of this kind of surprising expansiveness?

When Was the Last Time You Delighted in Something Ordinary Yet Beautiful?

The smell of grass soaked from a summer rain, crystals of frozen dew that change trees into sculptures of ice and light, or the intricate stitching of the handwoven rug beneath your feet afford you opportunities to be still for a moment, to receive, and to wonder. Think back to the past four or more days of such a time. Where were you? What senses were activated? In your Tracking Wonder notebook, list one small shift you could make to soak in a little more sensory delight.

What Activities or People Most Likely Foster More Wonder in You?

Your responses to the first two questions should provide clues to what you already do, where you go, and whom you're around when you're mostly like to experience these quiet yet crucial moments. Take one minute to take stock of them and list them—activities, places, and people. Now you have a starting list of what you could do or people you could be around more often to foster more daily expansiveness, delight, and elevation.

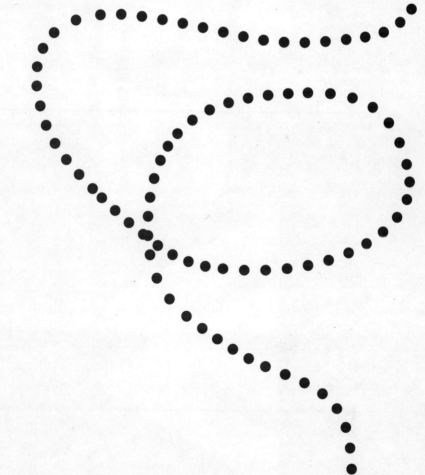

Wait.

are you bringing with you on this Tracking Wonder Journey?

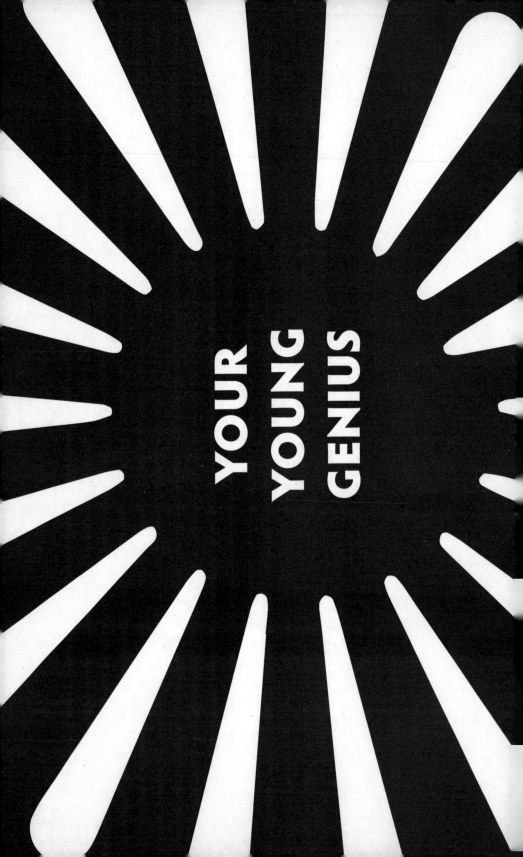

YOUR YOUNG GENIUS

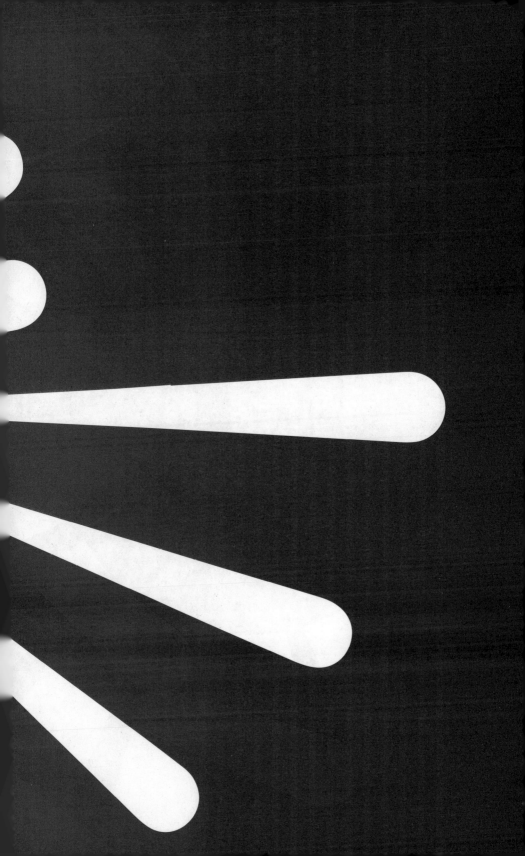

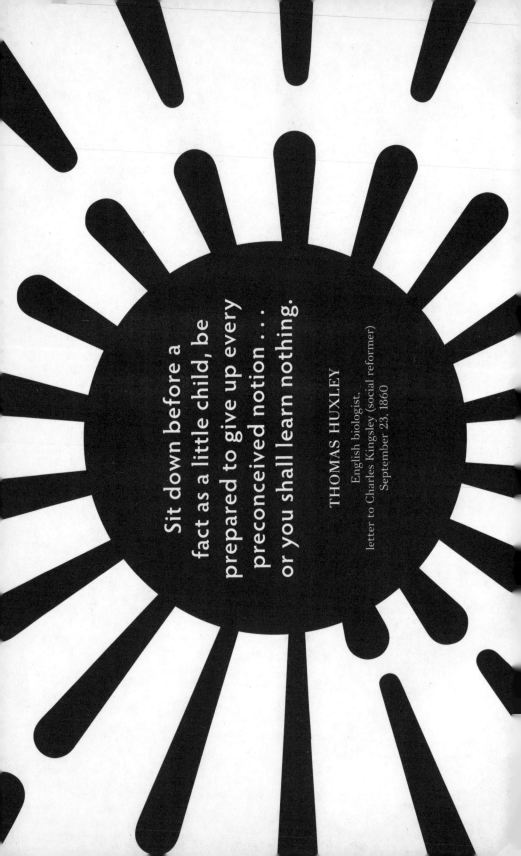

Sit down before a fact as a little child, be prepared to give up every preconceived notion . . . or you shall learn nothing.

THOMAS HUXLEY
English biologist,
letter to Charles Kingsley (social reformer)
September 23, 1860

WONDER WANES. WE KNOW THAT. Whether from human brains pruning their synapses by puberty, growing up amidst a productivity-centric society, or suffering from trauma, many adults have not retained their childlike openness, curiosity, and appreciation for the world's beauties. To survive, we become hardened realists and pragmatists. Yet—and this yet is important—we know deep inside that our capacity to experience wonder has not fully vanished because, upon occasion, we each do experience moments that astonish our soul.

How do we retrieve these youthful qualities without forsaking our worldly responsibilities? In my work of developing many methods to multiply these experiences, I've discovered a surprisingly effective answer to that question. To track wonder this way requires exploring your interior landscape in search of what I call your young genius—your most essential ally on this journey.

65

TRY THIS: "YOU ARE SEVEN YEARS OLD"

I know a lot of two-year-olds who have genius. They are terribly observant, absolutely curious, willing to take risks. . . . How to hold on to that native genius and also learn the things we need to survive?

ELLEN GILCHRIST

Pulitzer Prize–winning novelist, from her journals

Consider this scenario: You wake up one Monday morning to realize that your workday is cancelled. You have the day to yourself. What do you do? Where do you go? Whom do you see? If you're like most people, you might instantly list obvious obligations, such as working through your to-do list, taking care of other people's needs, and trying to be as productive as if you were doing a good job at work. Yes, the ethics of workism are deeply ingrained. But could we liberate our minds from these default patterns?

Psychologists Darya Zabelina and Michael Robinson of North Dakota State University set out to test a similar question. They knew certain things to be true based on their field's literature. Be more playful, and you're likely to come up with more novel and useful ideas (originality). Grow into an adult, and you're less likely to be playful. Two reasons: social obligations and your frontal cortex. As you mature, you develop a more sophisticated cognition and neurological wiring that makes you more self-conscious of

YOUNG GENIUS STORY

DENISE MARKONISH

senior curator and director of exhibitions at MASS MoCA, described by the *Boston Globe* "one of the country's most audacious curators"

I was somebody who liked to explore the world around me. I grew up in Brockton, Massachusetts, about a half hour outside of Boston, on a dead-end street in a neighborhood with a bunch of kids running around in the woods.

your obligations to others and possibly more guarded about other people's judgments of you. That's a one-two combination that nearly guarantees business as usual and life as usual. No surprise here, right? But Zabelina and Robinson wanted to know if grown-ups could cultivate a child-like mindset that would produce more original ideas.

They designed an experiment with seventy-six undergraduates. The control group was given a prompt similar to the one above. The other group was given the same prompt with one difference: They were told, "You are seven years old." You wake up one Monday morning to realize that your school day is cancelled. You have the day to yourself. What do you do? Where do you go? Whom do you see?

Could these five words—"You are seven years old"—make a difference in how you approach life? Each group was asked to write their responses to the prompt in specific detail. Here is an example from the control group: "I would go back to bed for a while if work was cancelled. I would then get up, check email, call work to see if they needed me to do anything there. . . . I then would go home to finish any homework or other things around my apartment." The other participants in the control group typically had these kinds of obligatory responses—finishing homework, going to work, checking email.

What happened with the group told to take on a seven-year-old's mindset? Here is an example: "I

> When I was young, I really wanted to be a geologist. I ran around filling my pockets with rocks, which I still do today. Even at a young age, I liked to organize things. I liked to build systems for these collections I would make.
>
> I've had a lifelong pursuit of wonder and curiosity. I've always been interested in knowing stuff, whether that was picking up a rock and trying to figure out what was in it or watching a cooking program and understanding how food was made. I just wanted to be a person who gathered information! That's still what I do.

would start off by going to the ice cream shop and ordering the biggest cone I could get. I would then visit the pet store and look at all the dogs. After that I would visit my grandma and play a few games of gin. Then she would make me cookies and give me a huge glass of milk. I would then go for a walk, where I would meet up with my friends and we would play in the park for hours." You can feel the difference. The seven-year-old embraces possibilities.

Between the adult mindset and the childlike mindset, who is going to have the more enjoyable, memorable, and meaningful adventure? More importantly, who is more likely to demonstrate agile problem-solving skills? I'd place my bets on the individual brimming over with seven-year-old vitality.

The scientists reported, "The written responses from the experimental condition were very different. They typically focused on desires rather than obligations." Before your rationalizing mind starts saying, "Yeah, sure, seven-year-olds have all the fun"—hold on. The point is not about wishing you were a child again or ignoring your real-world responsibilities. Instead, I'm curious how grown-ups can bring forward their best youthful attributes on their path to fulfillment.

If the study had stopped at comparing these written responses, the findings would be novel but not useful. This first written exercise is designed to establish a certain mindset. Writing, in other words, entrains a certain outlook. For example, if you were to write in specific detail about climbing a tree and swinging like a wild thing through the branches, you would awaken different parts of your brain and muscle memory associated with those activities than if you were asked to write about going back to bed or catching up on homework. In other words, writing from a seven-year-old's point of view itself primes a childlike mindset.

The next part of the study spelled out the key findings. With their mindsets primed as adult-like or childlike, members of the respective groups took a test with a set of tasks that the psychologists described as "arguably the gold-standard measure in the creative performance literature." Participants might be asked,

"Find an original use for a brick" or "What would be the strangest way to get out of bed?" or "Write an unusual title for the following story." When it comes to generating novel and useful ideas, those who adopted the seven-year-old's mindset outperformed those in the control group.

The scientists concluded that "it is possible to recapture the spirit of play and exploration characteristic of childlike thinking." They further noted that "thinking of oneself as a child, for a short period of time, appears to facilitate the sorts of playful, exploratory thinking processes conducive to creative originality."

Coming across this study was a watershed moment for me that corroborated a tracking wonder skill set. I previously had observed that the people who flourish over the long haul of a well-lived life maintain a healthy relationship with what I call their "young genius." What I share with you here is the basis for my trainings, teachings, and workshop experiences delivered to a wide berth of audiences as diverse as lawyers, start-up team members, city planners, and nonprofit executives.

But who is your young genius?

REMEMBER THE GENIUS IN YOU

We tend to associate genius with a very few lucky, gifted individuals. Let me clarify something: your young genius is a reflection of your inner gifts that evolves and re-emerges over the course of your lifetime. I do not use the word genius glibly. Indulge me here, then, in an etymological voyage, because I believe we modern English speakers have done the word genius a disservice. The idea of "genius" goes back to early civilization.

Genius was described by the world's first "positive psychologists"—the Western philosophical heavy-weights Socrates, Plato, and Aristotle. They, like us, were curious about what led certain people to flourish with their talent and lead fulfilled lives. They believed that all of us are born with a distinct force of character, a unique guardian attendant within. This force, beyond nature or nurture, was unique to the individual personality. Its presence within was to remind the person of their true nature or true calling in the world. This force of character in Greek is known as a *daemon*. A consistent translation of *daemon* is "genius." In Aristotle's descriptive study of how certain Athenians flourished throughout their lives, he observed that they consistently possessed *eudaemonia*—a set of activities that best brought forth the talents of their unique daemon.

Genius is that force of character that wakes you up to your best character and work in the world—if you awaken to it. When you experience *eudaemonia*, you feel more than "in flow." You feel as if most facets of your life align with your unique and greatest potential for fulfillment and contribution.

Here's the catch: We're born, so the Greek story goes, forgetting our unique nature, forgetting our genius. Yet we can remember it. Sometimes someone we trust mirrors back the genius

they see in us. But we also glimpse it when we engage in activities that bring our best talents and strengths alive—many times without regard for reward or recognition.

The first act you can take to bring your young genius on your tracking wonder journey is to *remember it*. If you regularly remember and recognize this force of character, it can guide you as you advance your best work and most meaningful life. I make that claim, again, based on my repeated—often weekly—experiences with the everyday and exemplary geniuses of creativity with whom I work. For a moment, it's as if you remember who you truly are.

Yet most often it is memories of your childhood—no matter the circumstances—that offer a glimpse into this unique force of character within you. Specifically, you can track moments of your youth

YOUNG GENIUS STORY

CHIP HEATH
coauthor of several bestselling books, including *Made to Stick*, and professor emeritus in the Stanford Graduate School of Business

I remember that at about seven or eight years old, I got my first manual typewriter, which was really cool. I just thought it was an extraordinary information-capturing device, and so I typed out a bunch of passages from nature books and created my own miniature encyclopedia. And I would walk around my apartment building with this thing, hoping that I would stumble across a situation that would be relevant for the interesting descriptions of monsters and exotic bears and stuff that I had typed into my word processor at the time, this manual typewriter.

when you felt most alive, open, and free to be your unique self. Those memories might take you back to your boundless enthusiasm at the cusp of a summer morning when you knew you were about to have a ton of fun—whether on a waterslide or in your own backyard. It was that dizzying feeling of limitless potential when you were immersed in the activity you would ultimately spend thousands of hours enjoying. For some people, that activity was learning to ride a bike or paint with watercolors, or maybe it was wandering the stacks of the library, following the rocky rolling path of a local creek, or playing your first competitive sport.

One modern-day Greek, Arianna Huffington, wrote about how she rediscovered her young genius. While researching a book about the gods of her homeland, she described how she found a forgotten part of herself that was a reflection of the mythic force of Hermes.

Within days of his birth, precocious Hermes was the only child god allowed among the other gods because of his spry cleverness—his special kind of genius. He could take a tortoise shell and transform it into a lyre, giving endless delight through beautiful music.

Reacquainting herself with this mythic story helped Huffington—then a middle-aged, high-profile wife of a battle-worn politician—reclaim her youthful spirit. She described her mentality in those days as "the need to control circumstances" and "to impose certainties in my life." But she said, "By rediscovering Hermes, I recreated his spirit: fluid, trusting, open to signs, coincidences, the unforeseeable, and the unexpected." A shape-shifter perennially open to clever play, Hermes is, Huffington writes, "the child that, if man is lucky, he never outgrows." The mercurial nature of Hermes liberated Huffington's playful side and allowed her to be more open to uncertainty as she reinvented herself many times over. She went on to found a media empire through her Huffington Post online platform that has empowered millions of people to think critically, embrace alternative lifeways, and live more fulfilled lives. Her most recent venture, Thrive Global, inspires leaders and workers to counter the notion that we must burn out as the price for success.

Huffington's example reinforces an important point: it is never too late to reclaim your young genius. Evelyn Asher is, as of this writing, an eighty-one-year-old member of the Tracking Wonder community and an active communications consultant. She told me that, as a child, she downplayed her creativity because her three brothers dubbed her "Miss Prissy" whenever she expressed her love of creative expression through writing poems or making plays that involved her friends. After holding positions in marketing and teaching communications courses, she started her own coaching and communications business at age seventy-six. Yet she grew frustrated whenever her business plans or events for executive women didn't pan out the way she wanted.

Then Asher became seven years old, so to speak, by actively reclaiming her young genius traits. "When I began to examine my efforts through the lens of my young genius," she told me, "I reintroduced my innate curiosity, love of creative expression, and desire to collaborate with others. I reimagined events with creative partners. It wasn't all about me or about outward success." She started experimenting with a collaborative effort called Wisdom Collective that invites women from many generations to engage in creative expression "adventures," both live and online. "I started photographing small wonders on my walks, like lampposts or train tracks. These images became clues to a mystery that then led to themes I would introduce to the Wisdom Collective." She soon assessed her efforts not through the bottom line but more by "how engaged people were and what lessons we all learned along the way." She now feels fulfilled, because "Miss Prissy" has evolved into a full-on curator of creative wisdom.

BRING YOUR YOUNG GENIUS TO WORK

Since 2010, I have tested out the idea of connecting many different audiences to their young geniuses. Without fail, it's an exercise that helps people get more comfortable with their creativity. I was once asked to work with a large group of executives and employees who worked with nonprofit donor foundations. Held two years after the Great Recession, the conference came at a time when most nonprofits were still recovering from the previous years' plummet in donations.

They were an eager group, though wary about creativity's value in such hard times, according to the organizer. This group was concerned with questions such as, "How do we hold better meetings?" and "What are we going to do about a personality clash between employees?" Imagine, then, how they responded when they entered the conference space and saw at the center of each table a set of crayons. One woman paused and muttered to her colleague, "Oh no. I hope we're not going to draw. I'm a horrible artist."

I never know how the group temperament will receive these ideas and activities related to tracking wonder. At times, my downer mind has imagined stories of outright mutinies among audiences—always a false narrative. Resistance, yes. Mutiny, no.

My presentation included interactive games to help them experience the neuroscience of creativity and the delight of active problem-solving. I also illustrated to them how certain nonprofits had flourished since the recession by using some of the principles we were considering.

At the peak of the workshop, they each creatively tracked a problem they perceived they had at work. For several minutes, they identified and defined their respective problem and analyzed in writing how they might go about resolving it. Standard stuff.

Then I asked them to stop, pause, and center. "Remember being seven years old," I said. Some squirmed in their chairs. Some grinned. "See yourself in one instance when you were at your creative best at age seven. Where are you? What and how are you creating? Who are you relating with and how? How do you stand out as a kid?" Tense jaws gave way to smirks and smiles. I asked them to write down three positive personality traits of themselves at that time. The room's curiosity quotient suddenly soared.

Then I suggested they forget their work-related problem for now and bring their seven-year-old

genius to the table. I displayed images from Maurice Sendak's classic children's book *Where the Wild Things Are*—a book that many of them remembered fondly from their youth. "Now, take your favorite-color crayon." They did so—including the woman who had groaned about her poor artistic talents. She was smiling. "Draw your own Wild Thing, a rule-breaking, fun-loving, wild-rumpus-throwing ally you'll bring to work with you. Forget talent or skill. Just draw with abandon and without regard for outcomes." Some dove in. Others delayed jumping in to choose exactly the right color

YOUNG GENIUS STORY

CHRIS FLINK
founding faculty of Hasso Plattner Institute of Design (Stanford's d.school) and CEO and executive director of the Exploratorium, a renowned museum of science, arts, and human perception in San Francisco

I think I maybe was at my best at eight. A lot of my career has been spent helping people recapture the curiosity and creative energy that they had at that age. I have certainly done my best to not relinquish it to the sort of adult systems that weigh upon us sometimes. When I think back to age eight, my joy was coming from trying to build tree houses and forts and booby traps, and drawing. I was often making things out of garbage, picking up weird pieces of packaging and turning them into spaceships or environments for my action figures and, I suspect, to assure their peers would not be judging their artwork. Within two minutes, the business-focused executives, administrators, and clerks were immersed in another place and time, on the page with color, imagination, and play. The vibe felt alive.

When I asked them to pause from drawing, there was a palpable groan. They wanted to keep coloring and playing. "We have work to do," I said, "but you can approach your problem now with a similar wild playfulness and openness." The exercise has the advantage of tripping up conventional ways of seeing, especially for those who tell themselves "I'm not creative."

or some other nerdy pursuit. I felt pretty uninhibited and very free just trying stuff, and imagination filled in all of the gaps for me. I think that sort of creative competency in young folks at that age is something all of us should try harder to recapture. It was about trying to make sense of the world and getting the greatest thrill in the moments where I felt some agency and some ability to shape parts of it, whether it was just a small corner on an awkward branch in a tree, or digging down in the earth and building a bunker, or making my own little fort out of blankets. I found a lot of joy in the power of directly affecting my own experience and creating an environment that I could share with my friends.

Next, I invited the group to return to their previous problem and approach it from a seven-year-old Wild Thing's point of view. To draw. To connect dots. To illustrate. To sketch prototypes. To name their solution. The room erupted in multiple exclamations of "Aha!" During our discussion, the conference organizer leaped to her feet to announce she had finally cracked a sticky problem by thinking in this new way. Others said they felt newly inspired. Afterward, a lawyer came up to me and, in a near-conspiratorial tone, confided that she felt something wake up in her. It was something she had not been able to admit to herself or to her colleagues who viewed her as the hard-hitting, relentless advocate for justice. "I think there's a part of me that's creative," she said, "but I don't always bring that part to work. I think if I did, I'd feel—I don't know—more alive or something." But she also expressed doubt. Was this a silly insight?

She wondered if it would be foolish to embody a seven-year-old's curiosity and enthusiasm in her legal pursuits. Her suspicions are warranted, of course. A thirty- or forty-something brings the weight of decades' more experience, sensibilities, and memories to any situation. We don't want to void our minds of personal cognitive history or else we *will* be foolish. Within any professional organization, some of us fear more than others the looming threat of how our colleagues will view us and whether or not we will be taken seriously. Still, when approaching any task for any purpose, you can ignite a youthful zeal by inviting your young genius to work with you.

The young genius intervention helps us see a part of ourselves that we want to see again. It also shows

our inner character without the grown-up context of performance or pay. We each have the capacity to bring the unique parts of our character to any project or problem.

What if, no matter our age or childhood circumstance, more and more of us grown-ups reclaimed our young geniuses? Might we collectively change the way we live, work, make, and love for the better? Let's visit Paris to find out.

YOUNG GENIUSES, UNITE

Genius is the capacity to retrieve childhood at will.

CHARLES BAUDELAIRE
poet and art critic

At around age sixty, Constantin Guys (pronounced GEES), a globe-trotting war correspondent, started gaining recognition not for his reporting but for his paintings. The self-taught artist did not hang out in Parisian salons or paint with oil, the medium of the masters of the time, but with watercolor. His subjects did not hearken back to romantic historical scenes or focus on larger-than-life heroes. Instead, his eye and brush and pencil captured ordinary women—from café-goers to prostitutes to women of "high society." It was the early 1860s in Paris, the world's art center. To most artists and art critics, Guys's work seemed crude. Yet the French poet and art critic Charles Baudelaire saw something refreshing in these colorful, gestural works. He used Guys's art as a focal point for a new point of view regarding what we would decades later call in the twentieth century "modern art."

In his essay "A Painter of Modern Life," Baudelaire wrote that Guys's earliest scribblings were so barbarian that "most of the people who know what they are talking about, or who claim to, could, without shame, have failed to discern the latent genius that dwelt in these obscure beginnings." *Latent genius.* Baudelaire noted that for over fifteen years Guys taught himself tricks of the trade while still being true to his own vision and sense of beauty. Isn't that the question for so many of us? How do we stay true to our original vision? How, as Ellen

Gilchrist asks, do we "hold on to that native genius and also learn the things we need to survive"?

What, then, is this innocent painter's special talent? Baudelaire describes Guys—and other such innovative artists—as similar to a child who possesses a ready openness and interest in surrounding things and people, no matter how ordinary or trivial. An innovative artist's special talent is that very childlike sensibility meshed with the grown-up's capacity for understanding and following through on a task.

"Genius is the capacity to retrieve childhood at will," Baudelaire announced. The capacity to retrieve childhood at will. Genius, like wonder, is an active trait, not an innate talent. You can track and foster wonder. You can create a new view of yourself and thus of the world around you.

In 1863, that statement would predict the quality of the most innovative painters, artists, and musicians to come over the next one hundred years—creatives such as Henri Matisse, Paul Klee, Joan Miró, John Cage, and Niki de Saint Phalle. Matisse, for instance, was so struck with the joy of life that this energy vibrates from his canvases.

His painting *Le bonheur de vivre* (1905) dissolved the conventional standards of technical virtuosity, perspective, and realism with simple nude forms lounging and dancing in a rainbow-hued outdoor setting that looked more like a psychedelic vision than a genteel tableau for the aristocracy. Critics railed. They could not tolerate the rule breaking. Yet Matisse prevailed. "You study, you learn," he said, "but you guard the original naiveté. It has to be within you, as desire for drink is within the drunkard or love within the lover."

And that original naiveté is within you. You were born with it. If you haven't guarded it much lately or in a long time, it's within you, too, to remember and reclaim that latent genius.

These artistic trailblazers showed the world how much power a youthful perspective can have to affect our emotions and even drive social change, leading to more and more innovators harnessing their childlike creativity. Over the past one hundred years or more, we have witnessed this youthful mindset as a through line in many fields—from poetry and jazz to philosophies of education and even a d -

YOUNG GENIUS STORY

JOHNATHAN FIELDS
host of the award-winning *Good Life Project* podcast, author of *Sparked*, maker, and dad

Our town, like a lot of small towns, had a town dump. And when I was eight or nine (and to this day) I loved to make stuff. I was also pretty obsessed with anything with wheels, which I liked to ride and make. I didn't come from a family where we had gobs of cash. If I wanted to make something, then very often I would have to figure out a way to get the parts. That led to me semiregularly begging one or both parents to drive the old Volvo down to the town dump and go

ver-
tis-
ing. It
would
have
seemed cra-
zy to propose
to nineteenth-cen-
tury physicists that
we would eventually travel
to the moon. It would have been
preposterous to 1960s librarians that much
of the world's knowledge would soon be available
on an interconnected global computer network. The
first hospital doctors would have found it inconceivable that children born with heart deformities
would lead healthy, active lives due to high-tech
medical advances.

searching for bike parts. We would sort of throw different things in the back and then
drive home. I would spend the next couple of days in the basement with random parts
and duct tape making Franken-bikes. There was a big rock down the road where all
of the kids hung out. It was kind of shaped like a small ramp. The goal was to see if
you could ride down the sidewalk on your bike as fast as possible, launch off the
rock, and fly in the air as many sidewalk blocks as you could. It was so fun
because when you did that on a Franken-bike, where you had like three
pairs of rusted-out forks duct-taped together to give you real chopper
style, there was a really good chance that the moment your
tires hit the ground, the entire thing would spontaneously
explode. That was the greatest payoff.

I
be-
lieve
that
o u r
ability to
remember
and reclaim
our respective
young geniuses holds
the key not to open-
ing us up to a more expansive
view of our own capabilities but also to
cracking us open to humanity's potential and advancing our culture at large. For you, this means
that no matter what age or stage you're at, waking
up your young genius can prove rewarding in all
your endeavors—personal or professional, creative
or cultural.

Look around you. The people you work with and for, the people you live with and love—do they not also each possess a distinct genius? What if you brought your genius to work with you every day, whatever the nature of your work in the world? What if you encouraged other people to do likewise? What ripples of impact could you begin?

As I write this piece this morning—almost as if on cue—my younger daughter slides open my studio door and brings me a peanut butter and banana smoothie. (Her name—Alethea—is Greek for "unforgetting." It relates to that moment when you un-forget or deeply remember the truth of your genius nature.) "Dahlia and I made these for breakfast," she says with her toothy grin. "We didn't have enough bananas for three, but here's a little of mine." Who would not welcome a genius interruption like that?

Your turn. Take a break. Choose wonder. And bananas.

YOUR YOUNG GENIUS

Maybe you feel as if you've forgotten your genius for, well, years. If so, that's okay. I've met and worked with many smart, accomplished people who feel similarly, at first. Be patient. This core part of your character is always within you, waiting to be recognized. It's a beautiful part of you that beckons you to be at your best, your most free, your most uniquely *you* in this one life. This Young Genius exercise is *the* quintessential exercise to launch your tracking wonder journey. It has four parts, and I suggest doing them in sequence to have the best results.

Part 1: Priming Exercise: Remember

Just as the "You are seven years old" study by Darya Zabelina and Michael Robinson demonstrated, writing with sensory detail for a few minutes

can help activate your imaginative memory. So if you're feeling in need of a creative warm-up, try this exercise first.

One of the most valuable tools to identify what might be your unique "genius" is to recall certain episodes from your youth in which you felt most free and at your best—without regard for external reward.

Regardless of circumstances—however good or bad—almost every child has the capacity to create their own sanctuaries of sorts. The beloved poet Mary Oliver noted that despite the trauma she experienced at the hands of her abusive father, she found solace in the woods and with words. Her genius may have initially led her to nature and writing for her own survival, but because she kept tending to her genius capacity to appreciate beauty, the result is a legacy of breathtaking poetry. No matter how harsh

Are you indoors or outdoors?
By yourself, with others, or with animals?

How do you feel in your body?
If you're communicating, how are you speaking in your unique way?

If you're doing an activity with others or in your surroundings, how are you doing so in your unique way?

or carefree, how dire or nondescript your childhood memories, there were moments at that age (I would wager) in which you felt free, alive, and truly yourself.

Imagine back to when you were young. With compassion, see your young genius possibly making or exploring or relating as only you seemed to do in your own way. Perhaps you had an idea to poster your walls with your artwork. Seeing how your brilliant images lit up the drab hallways, you got another idea to offer your art to your neighbors. And you went for it and brightened others' lives. Or maybe you set off into the woods to build a fairy hideout from evergreen branches and cardboard boxes. If you quiet yourself and allow your memory to take you back to such a moment, you will retrieve and remember a part of that genius character. If you find yourself inspired to revisit your genius at an older age, that's fine, too.

Check in.

Set a timer for four minutes and pick an episode that comes to mind. Simply begin by writing, or even sketching, if doing so activates your imaginative memory. When the alarm sounds, move on to the next step.

Part 2: Young Genius Traits: Recognize

Now, with compassion and appreciation, see and recognize that young genius's most distinct traits. Write down the three adjectives that describe your young genius.

1.

2.

3.

When I recall the long-haired towheaded boy I was, I see that boy roaming a wooded undeveloped lot up the road—a place of endless imaginings where he tried to talk to God, fly among birds, climb castle-like tree towers, and carve paths to other worlds. I see a boy writing in a notebook about his earliest memories, attuned to the unspoken feelings of other children and grown-ups. My young genius traits that I recognize almost every single morning in

my notebook these days are *Imaginative*. *Caring*. *Reflective*. These traits show up in my evolved grown-up genius often as *Forward-Thinking*. *Considerate*. *Reflective*. What are yours?

Part 3: Wild Thing: Activate

I invite you to imagine your Wild Thing, a fantastical reflection of your young genius. Try not to premeditate too much, and don't worry about artistic ability. The play's the thing. Get whatever art materials you have handy. You can start with the face. Maybe it has a certain kind of animal nose and another kind of beast ears. Maybe it has scales or fur, short hair or long scruffy dreadlocks or curly razzle-dazzle. Maybe its torso, legs, and feet come from another creature—a Komodo dragon, bird of paradise, or *Tyrannosaurus rex*? This thing has to be wild.

I'm serious about play. Why should you not be able to have a wild rumpus every once in a while with your projects? And if you're committing regular time to a new endeavor, you'd better be sure you're having more fun than frustration in the early stages.

Part 4: Bring Your Young Genius to Work: Reclaim

This final exercise encourages you to consider the practical ways you can invite your young genius to create with you. Take a moment to consider your projects or key activities over the past week or so. Go back through your calendar or planner if it helps jog your memory.

List three key activities you engaged in that you most enjoyed and that made you feel the most alive. How would you describe your personality in those moments? List three qualities.

How would you describe the way your mind works or the way you feel in those moments?

The Wild Thing of the author, whose genius claims no special artistic talent.

If I have written down my traits—*Imaginative. Caring. Reflective.*—then I scan my day's planned activities. I set a clearer intention, for instance, to show up with more imagination, caring, and reflection for an upcoming client meeting or a date with one of my daughters.

So much depends upon *who*—which *you*—you bring to work with you and on this tracking wonder journey. Whereas Charles Baudelaire notes that "genius is the capacity to retrieve childhood at will," I also suggest that genius is the capacity to reimagine and reclaim childhood at will.

Own the story of who you are as you keep your dream alive. You must rub the lamp for the genie to emerge.

Now, just be curious:
What activity can and will you do intentionally this week to bring out those personality traits? That activity could be something you do with your existing work. The activity could be related to your own idea, project, or endeavor that brings you meaning and sparks your creativity. The activity could be something new and distinct for your young genius. Perhaps you'll decide to go wading in a stream, coast down a hill on your bike, or spend a half hour sketching. Or maybe you'll decide to turn on some peppy music while filing reports, pause for a dance break while making dinner, or jump into the pile of leaves you just raked up.

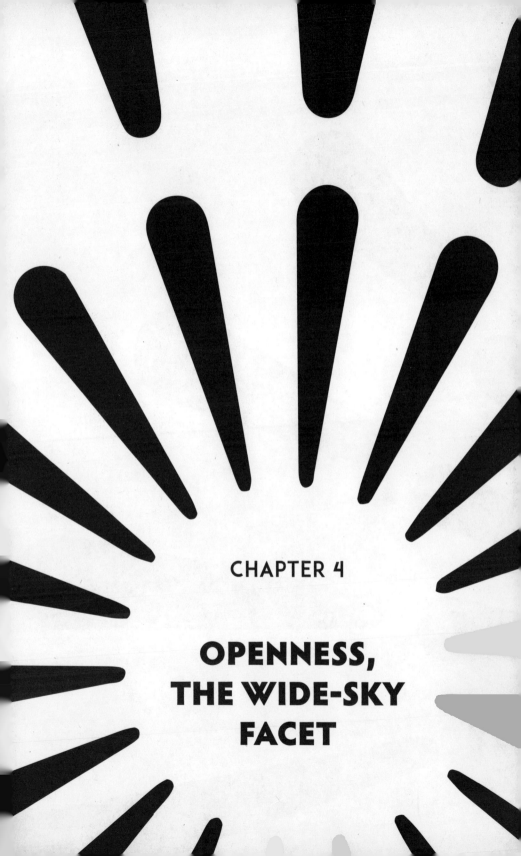

CHAPTER 4

OPENNESS,
THE WIDE-SKY
FACET

YOU MAY SAY I'M A DREAMER

WHEN MS. BURTON, MY high school drama teacher, informed our class we had to choose a song to sing as an audition for the spring musical, I nearly choked. The sole freshman among juniors and seniors, I was the one student who did not get tingly about song and dance on stage. How would I pull off a singing audition? My voice could crack at any second and break my brittle teenage ego. "Choose a song that means something to you" was the only direction I had. With no real musical knowledge, let alone voice training—save in the shower—and no friends "into" drama, I had no one to talk to about options. Neither parent would be much help either.

By the time I was a long-haired high school freshman, my parents had been divorced for almost two years. I had decided to live full-time with my bachelor dad in Fort Worth, Texas. Sentimental and generally jovial, my dad excelled as a media advertising and sales pro in Dallas—forty miles away—and that's where he spent much of his time. "Keep my trust, and you keep your freedom," he'd say on his way out the door a few times a week. I had ample time alone.

This was also the year that I messed up my high school course registration. With a few hundred students crammed into the school auditorium racing around signing up for classes, the chaos of the new environment distracted me, and I missed my opportunity to enroll in electives available to freshmen. I scrambled to fill my schedule and asked the stern-faced drama teacher if I could take her advanced class, even though I had zero experience with acting or singing in public. She grilled me on my commitment. Did I really have what it would take to shine in *advanced* drama? "Yes, ma'am," I said with actorly emphasis, and she reluctantly signed me up. I knew I had to live up to my word.

After the school bus dropped me at home one afternoon, I took off to my private spot to figure out what song to sing. Notebook in hand, I often walked my white German shepherd, Duchess, my steadiest friend at the time, down the road and behind the old schoolyard where I had attended elementary school. The school-yard opened onto a few remaining undeveloped acres with a rough path that led to an enclave of mesquite trees and juniper shrubs. This spot overlooked what felt to me like a tall cliff, but it was really the peak of a cutaway made for increasing traffic to pass through below. From my secret sanctuary—with my view elevated several yards above and across the boulevard, extending beyond the rail-road tracks and stretching onto still more wooded acres that had so far escaped the sight of hungry developers—I could gaze out at an open horizon. I lacked the emotional vocabulary to grasp what had happened to our fragile family, and something else inside me was changing. I couldn't envision a better future. I could only feel some dim sense of loss of my boyish enthusiasm to imagine a tree as a shipwrecked vessel, to build a fort from downed branches, to travel into a world of my own making. "I am losing my imagina-tion," I had written in my notebook around that time. Adulthood, like some uninvited development, lurked on the horizon.

With Duchess resting by my side as cars hummed below, I won-dered about that boy. Before me for as far as my wide eyes could see, only trees; and above me, only sky. *Only sky.* Yes. And then I knew the song.

Several days later I arrived at drama class timid but ready. Once Ms. Burton gave us our order of auditions, she propped herself behind a piano to accompany us one at a time. First up, Katie, a senior, harmonized "Day by Day" from *Godspell* in a way that made my heart swell to the ceiling. Raymond, also a senior, belted out a rousing performance of "Ya Got Trouble" from *The Music Man*, complete with hand gestures and staging. Then it was my turn. I handed the teacher the sheet music. She grew quiet. "Well, okay," she said. "This is not a standard musical number, but I think we can make it work." She looked me straight in the eyes. Maybe for the first time she glimpsed beyond my feathered bangs to see the shy, earnest dreamer inside me. "You give it your best, Jeff," she said and almost smiled. "That's all I ask."

For the next three (excruciatingly) long minutes, that's what I did. I closed my eyes and found a place within that touched the loss I felt for the full houses of friends and family during the holidays, of wild days roaming the woods in play instead of worry, of some ideal world beyond hate and harm, of some capacity to feel love. I sang, the best I could, the plaintive "Imagine" by John Lennon.

On the last line—"And the wor-rld will live as one"—I opened my eyes and saw Katie, whose eyes teared up. Raymond grinned with approval. Ms. Burton smiled and said, "That was beautiful." And they applauded. For a moment, among the older, more talented kids, I belonged. (And, thank goodness, my voice didn't crack.)

A couple of the seniors, including Katie, befriended me. Three years older, she seemed vastly wiser and safer to talk with than any of my friends, whose main mode of talking in those days was barbed sarcasm. In the audience seats one night, while we watched the rehearsals, I confided in her about how awkward I felt in the class and about my cringe-worthy audition song. She listened and told me how she and most of her friends were consumed with getting accepted into college, trying to figure out where they were going with their lives—something that seemed worlds away from my reality. She said something to the effect of, "When you sang that song, I think you reminded some of us of our own dreams. That's important." It was possibly the most profound thing anyone had ever told me.

And that's what I want to say to you. Remind yourself of your own ideals and dreams. It is more than okay to be an idealistic, wide-eyed grown-up in a world where cynicism comes easily. It is necessary. When you do so, you remind others around you that dreaming is important, too. Whether you, like some of my clients, can imagine what it would be like to create a game café, convert a three-hundred-year-old property into a CBD farm, or create more joy in your home and family, a space as wide as the sky to dream can fuel you with audacity.

Dreams begin in wonder, but sometimes it takes a song and a nudge and a little naiveté to keep them alive.

FACET 1: OPENNESS

When I look back on my youth and young adulthood, I see myself as mostly nonjudgmental and radically receptive to other people and new experiences. I was unsophisticated, with a sort of dreamy openness. My head was decidedly often in the clouds. "If you have built castles in the air, your work need not be lost," Henry David Thoreau once wrote in *Walden*. "There is where they should be. Now put foundations under them."

As an adult, I have since learned many practices to anchor my feet on the ground while relearning how to bring dreams to fruition. I find it fortunate that I have not lost that naive edge while still allowing other parts of me to mature. I've learned not only how to balance financial books and be fully present-minded but also how to build successful programs that have benefited thousands of people. Think of the refrain in David Byrne's song "This Must Be the Place (Naive Melody)": "Head in the sky, feet on the ground." Both, together, make up an *intelligent* naiveté.

In the early 1990s, the renowned psychologist Mihaly Csikszentmihalyi (pronounced cheeks-SENT-me-high) and his team interviewed ninety-one people who have made notable innovative contributions to their respective domains—business, the sciences, the arts, government. Each of these scientists, doctors, poets, painters, climbers, and inventors was at least sixty years old. Csikszentmihalyi's findings revolutionized the field of psychology by tracking people's immediate direct emotional responses while they were immersed in deep experiences of fulfillment—experiences that he named "flow." Among his many notable findings that he presented in his follow-up study on creativity is that a creative person tends to maintain a complex personality. By complex, Csikszentmihalyi specifically meant that these creative contributors "contain contradictory extremes."

He wrote that creative people "tend to be smart, yet also naive at the same time." Csikszentmihalyi noted what many psychologists have since confirmed: intellectual intelligence beyond a base-level competency neither correlates with high creative output nor with a fulfilled life. Perhaps people with high IQs are able to master the conventional, crystallized thinking of any domain, yet they have little incentive, Csikszentmihalyi speculated, to be curious, "to question, doubt, and improve on existing knowledge." This is probably why the German poet Goethe wrote that "naiveté is the most important attribute for genius."

Did you catch that? *The most important attribute for genius is naiveté.* Remember, when we track wonder, we question the notion that only some people have genius, and we revive the idea of the Greek daemon, the inner force of genius within everyone.

Openness meshed with this intelligent naiveté is the first facet of wonder we'll track together. Far from indicating amateurism, this quality helps you experience anew the world within and around you, giving you an advantage with your creative endeavors and imbuing your life with more meaning. As recent studies have corroborated, your openness to experience, more than your intellect or other factors, could better indicate your ability to find creative solutions to problems, big and small. Openness, like a wide-open sky, can keep awakening you to what is possible in this one life.

INTELLIGENT NAIVETÉ AT WORK

Openness can boost your on-the-job creativity and fuel you to pursue your dream in a way that only you can do. Just ask my favorite entrepreneur of cooling equipment, Carey Smith, an adventurer and everyday genius of creativity. In fact, Smith was not afraid to make an ass of himself when he renamed his second business, originally called HVLS Fans. The "HVLS" stood for high-velocity, low-speed—a description for the kinds of fans once relegated to overheated factories, auto shops, and airless government buildings. While some hard-line, bottom-line CEOs might let profits and safe strategies drive the business, Smith's idealism drove his. One of his genius traits is listening to and taking care of people. In the early years of HVLS Fans, as profits lagged, he'd receive calls from people asking, "Are you the guys who sell those big-ass fans?" and "Are you that big-ass fan guy?"

Smith listened and changed the business name: Big Ass Fans. During the Great Recession, Big Ass Fans could have followed its competitors either into bankruptcy or selfishness. Without a moral compass anchored in possibility and idealism, Smith could have made some bad moves. Instead, he kept his eyes wide and his heart open. While his more conservative competitors laid off employees and tightened funds, Smith kept every employee at some of the state's most competitive wages and gave them bonuses. His competitors went lean and invested in tight systems; Smith went human and invested in the right people. His competitors went public; he stayed private with an employee profit-share model. His competitors' personae appear clean and impersonal; Smith calls himself the "Chief Big Ass" instead of the CEO. Not wanting customers to get the wrong idea about what their name means, they made a large donkey their mascot.

His competitors invested in efficiency; Smith invested in excellence. Smith's eye for beauty converted a product once relegated to factories into functional art objects. Smith's Big Ass fans became essential in Hollywood celebrities' homes, movie sets, and chic restaurants. In short, Smith made big fans hip.

The payoff? From 2008 to 2010, his company's sales jumped 47 percent to $49.7 million. The next year, sales jumped another 41 percent to $70 million. By 2014, sales had reached $175 million, and in 2019 he sold Big Ass Fans for $500 million. He went from zero up to a Silicon Valley level of valuation, but Smith wasn't chasing unicorns. He was after mastery and meaning. And before he became virtuosic, he had to leverage his naiveté. His openness to possibility, his artfulness, and his idealism have given him a meaningful, creative life committed to excellence.

When Smith started his first business, which manufactured rooftop fire sprinklers, he said he knew absolutely nothing about what he was doing in business. That naiveté gave him an advantage, he believes. If he had known the challenges he was in for, he might have never gone for it.

Let's pause here for a moment. This is something I've heard from many entrepreneurs, professionals, and first-time authors—people who venture into terra incognito. Their lack of knowledge—their *ignorance* of the hurdles they would face in business or in creative pursuits was to their advantage. Why? Because they did not know what to fear, so they simply approached every step along the way with fresh eyes.

Let me reiterate that discovery: Sometimes *not knowing* what to fear is advantageous. Framed another way, consider what Ray Dalio, founder of the assets management firm Bridgewater Associates and the seventy-ninth wealthiest person in the world, says about his success: "Whatever success I've had in life has had more to do with my knowing how to deal with my *not* knowing than anything I know."

Therein is part of the paradoxical space that tracking wonder holds. Tracking wonder, as we will see repeatedly, keeps disrupting what we think we know.

Openness primes us to tolerate uncertain outcomes. To take risks creatively doesn't mean you gamble your life savings on a marketing scheme. It means you're willing to invest time, resources, and cognitive energy into a dream that has an uncertain outcome. Maybe you've figured out a way to make new yummy flavors of ice cream with organic ingredients, but you have no idea how to make a business of your idea. Tracking this facet of wonder suspends the requirement for immediate answers in favor of the process of figuring things out. Instead, wonder asks, "What might happen next?"

BUILD YOUR CASTLE WITH IDEALISTIC BRICKS

Carey Smith's example illustrates how we can lead our lives with our ideals instead of with conventional safe bets. Let's consider what happens when you want to pursue a dream—whether it is to create an exploratorium-like bedroom for your child or to advance your ambitious mission to recycle plastic into school building bricks (like Conceptos Plásticos, founded in Columbia). Maybe your downer voice says to you, "That will never happen. Why even try?" If your attention is consumed with worry, fret, or even hyper-busyness, your awareness narrows. When that happens, parts of your brain activate that also limit your mind's ability to generate novel and counterintuitive approaches to your dream.

Imagine your mind like a house with many windowed rooms. If you keep stuffing that house with more boxes of knowledge to prop yourself up like an expert in disguise, soon those windows will get blocked. You won't be able to look out toward a horizon of possibility. If you hear a voice telling you that you don't know enough to start your own school or your own product line of journals, do like Smith and listen to your young genius. Take stock of your dream of what could be, even if it does, as Thoreau suggested, seem like a castle in the air. Imagine every open action you take toward your dream as laying down a brick imbued with your intelligent idealism. That's business as unusual.

Now let's consider the opposite attitude and disposition for a moment so we can better track the facet of openness.

DROP THE COOL: SURVIVAL OF THE OPENNEST

Cultural attitudes can influence just how comfortable we are with being open in the world. I once had a journalist friend who loved to drop names and trends. Almost every time we got together, she'd work in a reference to an obscure but "brilliant" musician she'd interviewed, or she'd tell me how a recent exhibit at the Museum of Modern Art was noble but fell short of expectations. She was a connoisseur of an in-the-know culture. She always regaled me with riotous (if not gossipy) tales of traipsing around with creative celebs, but after a few years, I noticed the tone of our conversations shift. Fewer musicians that she spoke of were so-called brilliant and more of them were just industry hacks. In her view, the art world had become full of phonies who knew more about investing than they did about real art. Her former air of sophistication had collapsed into a trough of cynicism.

Sometimes sophistication and cynicism overlap. And sometimes, depending upon whom you hang out with, it's hard to see beyond the walls of sophistication or cynicism to glimpse another view of reality. Different from those skeptical of mistruths, cynical people can appear highly competent, and by criticizing idealism they can exude a worldly air. "Been there, done that, nothing can impress me" is what a cynical outlook often expresses. That attitude convinces a lot of people of the inherent futility of any creative or fulfilling pursuit.

Have you ever curbed your enthusiasm or hidden your naiveté for fear you might appear foolish? Maybe you have absorbed a belief that most people are self-interested and that you shouldn't trust their motives. Do you think that to be taken seriously and "make it" in the world, you must become competitive, shrewd, and guarded? Or if you haven't internalized these messages, you might have regarded yourself as weak, ignorant, or missing the "survival-of-the-fittest gene." Rest assured, I have had many clients—some of them executives and successful professionals—who have had to question their cynical beliefs. Teams and leaders I've worked with often want to bypass any hint of exhibiting qualities of a dreamer. They hear and preach: *Be smart. Be aggressive. Appear smart. Appear aggressive.* Unfortunately, I've also seen leaders shout down a potentially viable idea *too soon*. It's understandable why we want to appear certain. When uncertainty or unbidden surprises arise, an alert signal goes off in the brain. We're wired to quickly make unfamiliar objects and ideas familiar so we can "get on with the day." Cognitive psychologists call this tendency "the familiarity bias." Yet, although cynicism masks itself as sophistication and superiority, it is a form of rigid thinking.

Imagine you could disrupt your default cynicism. What if, like Carey Smith, you could lead your life based more on your idealism than on a desire to appear cool or at least not foolish? What would it take to approach challenges with more openness instead of with a default negative assumption? Yes, we are all haunted by nightmare scenarios, real and dreamed, but to increase your ability to track wonder, you can give those scenarios less weight in your decision-making.

The good news is we can break the spell of cynical, conditioned reactivity with practice. With a bit of mental window opening, an irritation or a doubt could be an opportunity to solve a common problem in an uncommon way. Here's another fun wordplay for this practice: Rearrange the letters of *reactivity* and you can spell *creativity*. That's a kind of spell you can cast on your outlook more often than you might think.

If you think you were born cynical and reactive, think again. The humanistic psychologist Scott Barry Kaufman is the former scientific director of the Imagination Institute in the Positive Psychology Center at the University of Pennsylvania, the author of *Wired to Create* and *Transcend: The New Science of Self-Actualization*, and the host of the number one psychology podcast in the world—*The Psychology Podcast*. For several years, he's been tracking the correlations among intelligence, imagination, and creative achievement. "Visionary tech entrepreneurs, world travelers, spiritual seekers, and original thinkers of all types," Kaufman says, "tend to have highly open personalities." People with this openness are adventurers—but not always of the Indiana Jones variety. These creative trailblazers might check off their bucket lists swimming the Atlantic on New Year's Day and flying in a hot-air balloon over Hawaii's Waipi'o Valley, both outward experiences, but they also relish exploring new ideas and possibilities, inward experiences. Openness to new experiences, as Kaufman's findings on this facet show, is something we can cultivate. Assuming an open and creative mindset means you can approach each day and situation in a fresh way. You're able to question your own assumptions and interrupt your own preconceptions. Even when you're tired or discouraged, a creative mindset keeps opening you up to what's possible.

SMILE TO SEE THE FOREST

One beautiful outcome of my tracking wonder has been to bring me back to my body. My conversation with Dacher Keltner, for instance, helped me connect dots between a state of openness in mind and in body. By title, Keltner is a professor of psychology at UC Berkeley as well as the founder and director of the Science Center for the Greater Good. But in spirit, Keltner is a true wonder tracker. Keltner's body of work has helped drive an increasing appreciation for how awe enlivens and elevates us. In a conversation many years ago, he described how for decades psychologists have detailed the physical signs of certain emotional experiences. For instance, in an experience of wonder, the eyes often dilate, the mouth might open, the vagus nerve connecting the mind and the heart might be activated.

That conversation with Keltner led me to practice a method of diagnosis with people I worked with. How can we know if we are functioning in a closed or an open state? Keltner's and other psychologists' work—even going back to Charles Darwin—had focused on observing how emotional states provoke physical responses. More recent studies, though, have focused on whether you could practice the opposite pathway and induce a positive emotional experience through a physical one. One study showed, in short, that the one factor that broadened participants' minds was genuine smiling.

The following contrast is not precise, nor are "closed states" mutually exclusive from "open states," but this chart can help you begin to track this facet of openness in your mind-body-heart.

Our work here is observing how we can actively foster openness—even when we *think* we don't feel like it. Both closed and open states can serve their roles in our creative well-being, but chances are, without periodically pausing to track this facet of wonder, you might pass through more of the day in a closed state than you realize.

A Closed State Feels Like	An Open State Fees Like
Eyesight narrowed	Peripheral vision expanded
Muscles around the temple, neck, shoulders and stomach tightened	Muscles relaxed and breathing eased

A Closed State Thinks Like	An Open State Thinks Like
Getting things done	Playing
Persisting with what is known	Exploring possibilities
Commanding	Listening and asking

OPEN YOUR EYES

You can practice seeking novelty through your perception of what's familiar right around you. Remember that one of the qualities of wonder, as opposed to awe, is the fact that wonder sneaks into the creases and cracks of everyday life. It doesn't have to be ignited by fireworks and waterfalls. When you open your eyes to wonder, you can see unexpected connections—*if* you practice recognizing them.

What if you stopped to appreciate how a tree might be shaped like an umbrella or how an umbrella might look like a question mark or how a question mark might appear like a leaping dancer? Could you take delight again in your natural ability to see the world's disparate things as interconnected? Yes, you could. So much is possible. Think of the Chilean Nobel Prize–winning poet Pablo Neruda writing an ode to a worn-out pair of socks, or designers who convert plastic waste into useful objects, or your own ability to find a new use for an old kitchen utensil. The ordinary becomes extraordinary. Experiences of wonder, in other words, disrupt our preconceived ways of viewing our environment and, in turn, ourselves.

You also can practice widening your eyesight by finding a horizon. Since I was a teenager seeking a song, I've been drawn to horizons. I often wonder if vistas and vast horizons magnetize us not only for their beauty but also for what they awaken in us—namely, an openness to possibility. Our eyesight and metaphorical vision expand. As we stand in one spot on land and gaze out toward another spot where earth or water or urbanscape meet air, it's as if our present spot is drawn out from our heart to the horizon where we could be. It's stretching out from presence to possibility.

One study published in *Evolutionary Psychology* found that rivers and beaches consistently elicited in subjects high feelings of fulfillment and low levels of isolation, but mountaintops and forests could elicit either elevation or apprehension.

Not everyone has a view from a mountain or out over an ocean a few minutes' drive away, but there is always some place to access a horizon, even if you have to climb to a rooftop or borrow the view of a corporate hotel. When one of my clients in Manhattan wanted to explore a whole new way of working beyond her practice to more of a public thought leader and mentor, it felt risky to her. As beautiful as her office was, her eyes needed relief from her inner walls. So for a few weeks, she would take a walk every Friday afternoon to view the Hudson River at a particularly scenic spot. There, the breeze and sun softened her tough gait built up from so many years arguing tough cases. Watching so many people enjoying the city reminded her of the promise of New York: if you can make it there, you can make it anywhere, as the saying goes. She said she could feel the tension in her head and shoulders dissolve. Visiting the pier and letting her eyes stretch out to another horizon put her in a more open disposition. Afterward, she said she was better prepared emotionally, mentally, and physically to make the changes necessary both within herself and within her practice to fulfill her new calling.

An open attitude means you take a dream seriously and *yet* you also find ways to enjoy the journey. The psychiatrist Nancy C. Andreasen, who studies creativity and the brain, knows this is so. One of the first neuroscientists to use advanced imaging technologies to study brain functioning, Andreasen wrote that "the capacity to approach the world in a playful and even childlike manner adds an intermittently joyous tone to the life of the creative person." And humor and playfulness—as Chief Big Ass Carey Smith's example illustrates—make the whole endeavor more enjoyable and fulfilling for everyone involved.

DRIVING THROUGH WOW!

One summer I went in search of wonder, fully anticipating the joy and fulfillment a trip to the Southwest would be. At the time, it seemed like a great idea to ask my new girlfriend to join me. Excited about each other, we both loved to travel, and I had a quirky passion I wanted to pursue. A few hours in, with our sweaty backs glued to the car's crammed bucket seats and the heat of the day torching us from every angle, I started to question my judgment. It was the first summer Hillary and I dated, and I had asked her to join me in Taos, New Mexico, at the end of a five-day course I was teaching at a conference on "writing into wonder." Our plan was to travel through the State of Enchantment and into Texas's Panhandle to track Georgia O'Keeffe's early footsteps there in the early twentieth century as a teacher, administrator, and artist. I had been geeking out on O'Keeffe research because I loved the artist's work and bold way of tackling life. Despite the rules imposed on her as an educator (Why can't she teach barefooted?) and the neighbors' raised brows at the woman dressed in all black, her letters from the time constantly reference wonder, especially toward Canyon, Texas's expansive, ocean-like prairies and skies. "SKY!" she exclaimed in one letter to her friend, Anita Pollitzer. "You have never seen SKY—it is wonderful."

I wanted to experience this sky for myself. Rather than rent a car on-site, the plan was for Hillary to drive my aged green Chevrolet Cavalier—the Cucumber, we called it—from New York to Taos, and then join me as I tracked down a few leads I'd come up with in my research—relatives or people with memories of young O'Keeffe. We would camp in Palo Duro Canyon where the painter often traveled with one of her younger male students to paint what would become some of her signature canvases. I thought I had a chance of finding that now-elderly male student who had proposed marriage to O'Keeffe. What could go wrong?

Well, on second thought, it seemed risky to bring Hillary. Accustomed to traveling solo, I knew that things never went to plan, and I didn't want to disappoint her or compromise our new relationship. On our first day out to find a camping spot in New Mexico's Carson National Forest, the temperature climbed into the high nineties. The Cucumber had no working air conditioning—a fact I had never bothered about in New York's Hudson Valley, which now seemed like an embarrassing oversight. I gripped the steering wheel but tried to relax my shoulders and force an easeful smile. Hillary must have sensed my chagrin. We kept quiet for the first hour or so.

And then we hit the highway toward the Rio Grande Gorge, an eight-hundred-foot chasm, and there we were—Hillary's long hair blowing from the open window, and for miles upon miles in all conceivable directions flat land stretched toward a rim of mountain ranges between the earth and sky encircling us. At that moment, something dissolved between Hillary and me, between my body and the car and the road and the land and the sky. The whole swirl of the universe compacted in those few seventy-miles-per-hour seconds. *Wow!* I not only wanted to say. *Wow!* I not only felt swirl through my body. But *Wow!* I sensed we were rocketing through one vast O shape of this parcel of earth, the shape of my eyes absorbing this openness, the shape of a mouth rounded out in awe. Anxiety flew out the window. We were in Wow!

At one point, Hillary looked over at me and said, "Jeffrey, I just want you to know that I have no expectations. I am completely open to whatever happens." What a wonder tracker! That initiation of the trip, fraught with 105-degree weather in Texas and a series of chance and oft-failed leads (maybe I'll detail them one day) ultimately built our trust in each other and kept us open to possibility.

In these moments of wonder, something in the flesh and mind drops its guard and you experience *radical* openness, the sort of receptivity that unravels your assumptions about what is possible.

In these moments of wonder, something in the flesh and mind drops its guard and you experience *radical* openness, the sort of receptivity that unravels your assumptions about what is possible.

This openness is available to you, wherever you are. Imagine.

OPENNESS

You can start tracking your own openness and intelligent naiveté by taking a few deliberate actions and noting your response to them.

Visit a New Place at Least Once a Month

If you find yourself in a rut of daily routine, try this invitation. A lesser-known art gallery or art museum is a good place to start. "Lesser-known" because you might attend with fewer expectations. If there's a college nearby, see if their art museum has an upcoming student exhibition. College art students can be especially experimental, daring, and unrefined. Seeing young artists' work or the early work of renowned innovators reminds me of that creative daringness within all of us.

When I lived in Dallas in my twenties, I would take off every few months for a weekend to a remote small town with two purposes in mind: to get a sense of the people, and to find the quietest spot in nature. I discovered that there are *hundreds* of Texases, not just one monoculture prone to stereotypes. You can visit an online map of your region and see what places on the map are within an hour's drive.

Pursue a Hobby with Abandon

The word *amateur* comes from the Latin *amatore*, meaning "lover" (as in *amore*). An amateur is not a hack but someone who has an unbridled enthusiasm for something. If you like doing activities with others, there are lots of organizations for amateur astronomers, woodworkers, photographers, musicians, and others. I've taken up stonework recently to learn to make stone paths, stone benches, and a new fire pit for our home. Doing so humbles me by exposing me to what I do not know and am unskilled at, but when I learn a new skill, it stretches my mind and gives me satisfaction. These are the types of small wins that ultimately build our confidence for achieving our bigger goals. And wonder accompanies the process.

Find a Horizon

When you feel closed down or simply in need of an open perspective, your eyesight could use topographical inspiration. A simple yet effective way to track this kind of visual openness is to find your horizon spot where you can gain a big visual expanse. Find a place that's easy to access and makes you feel open, elevated, and positive.

Take your Tracking Wonder notebook with you. When you arrive at your horizon spot, secure a place where you can stand or sit comfortably for several minutes without much distraction. Ground down in your seat or stance by scanning your surroundings and feel its presence. *You are here.* Acknowledge your life, work, or endeavor as it is. Express gratitude for what is here.

Now position your body so you can gaze directly onto the physical horizon before you. Imagine that the line from your heart to the horizon is like a near-future timeline of the coming months or year.

With a steady gaze upon the future horizon, permit yourself to dream, *really* dream. See yourself creating anew—a part of your life, a part of your work, a new program or aspect of your business. Envision yourself engaged regularly with one or more people, a project, or activities that bring you fulfillment.

Imagine yourself taking actions now that get you closer to that future horizon. When you notice fears surface, keep reminding yourself simply to dream and imagine. Capture in your notebook any images, phrases, words, or insights that arise.

These inquiries can spur your wondering:

What will you create and how will you be creating differently in the coming months?

How could what you create influence other people for the better?

How will your life have even more meaning and fulfillment?

How are your present mindset and actions getting you closer to that horizon?

You may find that one or more of these invitations becomes a new routine for you and gives you that unexpected Wow! moment. May it be so.

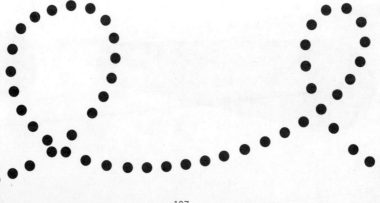

CHAPTER 5

CURIOSITY,
THE REBEL
FACET

THE WORLD IS BIG

CRISTIAN FRACASSI NEVER THOUGHT his curiosity could save lives. Fracassi, a civil engineer with a PhD in polymer science (plastics), lives in Brescia, Italy. Early in Italy's 2020 pandemic lockdown, the coronavirus had struck especially hard at a nearby hospital. To keep patients alive, they needed special valves for respirators, but the valve manufacturer couldn't meet the demand quickly enough. The valve connects the patient to the ventilator and mixes filtered oxygen with air. Each valve must be replaced for each patient. The design is quite complex because the hole through which the oxygen diffuses is less than a millimeter in diameter. Fracassi and his business partner Alessandro Romaioli wanted to help with what they had—namely, a 3D printer and their experimental wits. The problem? Their five-year-old company had only made practical objects such as bicycles and silicon bandages, not life-saving valves.

"We were very afraid," Fracassi told me by email. "We never had to design so quickly (in less than eight hours), and we had never designed anything that could save human lives." How do you overcome those fears when lives are literally at stake?

First, when they visited the hospital and saw firsthand the doctors' desperation, Fracassi said, "We just tried to trick our minds and put aside fear to try to help." Their first attempts weren't quite right, but they kept working until they had what seemed like a viable prototype—an imperfect but testable form. A doctor then tested the four valves, provided free of charge. The two engineers stayed in the corridor for what seemed like an interminable half hour until at last the doctor came out, expressionless. For a few seconds, they feared failure. The doctor finally announced, "It works." An "exaggerated joy" overcame them. Then the doctor asked for one hundred more valves, an order they promptly filled. All free of charge.

Then Fracassi and Romaioli did something else beautiful. They made the "blueprint" open-sourced and downloadable for anyone—with the legal caveat that these valves were temporary and to be used only for emergencies. When I asked Fracassi how this experience felt, he said, "When people send us a message saying 'Thanks to you, one hundred people breathe,' it is better than receiving the Nobel Prize. It makes you feel alive. It makes you feel useful to the world."

Support poured in from organizations, universities, and people from around the world. Multinationals such as Ferrari, Mercedes, and General Motors, as well as universities such as Stanford, Columbia, and Harvard extended their financial support and encouragement.

"We have discovered that the world is big," Fracassi told me, "and it is a friend when you try to do good instead of just fixate on making money." The world is big. That discovery, of course, is a moment of open, perhaps naive, wonder that defies the cynical or defeatist view of reality. Fracassi sees the world as brimming with beautiful possibilities. That's what can happen when you pursue your curiosity.

YOUNG GENIUS STORY

CRISTIAN FRACASSI
named by Fortune with his business partner, Alessandro Romaioli, as one of the "25 World's Greatest Leaders: Heroes of the Pandemic"

I have always been a very curious person since I was a child. I stayed with my grandmother many days while my parents worked. My grandmother called me Mike Buongiorno, a famous TV host who died years ago. He was a great talker, and I was never silent. My favorite question was "Why?"— Why does Mom work? Why does the dog sleep? Why does the wheel turn? Why does the water boil? Why? Why? Why? Many times, my grandmother couldn't answer, and when my parents came back to pick me up, I did the same thing with them by constantly asking questions. My dad was good at doing everything—fixing machines, restoring antique furniture, making gardens, cutting bonsai, painting; and I was always at his side and learning with my own eyes.

FACET 2: CURIOSITY

Fracassi's story and disposition show how a curious nature and creative mindset can drive our quest for a fulfilling life. Recent studies, such as those by the psychologist Todd Kashdan, have corroborated that people with high curiosity day in and day out report higher levels of life satisfaction, well-being, and meaning. Something else about this investigative force within us makes it especially relevant. As Mihaly Csikszentmihalyi, whom we discussed in the previous chapter, notes, "Without a burning curiosity, a lively interest, we are unlikely to persevere long enough to make a significant contribution." Isn't that what we each hunger for—for our lives to make some contribution, however big or small, to this world? If done beautifully, cultivating curiosity means that we live with more wondrous questions than definitive answers. Curiosity is another facet of wonder we can track. It is a proactive, playful mindset that urges us to pursue discovery, seek new knowledge, keep learning by doing, and question the status quo.

WONDER IS THE MOTOR OF HUMAN LEARNING

One of my clients, a consultant who develops leadership potential in universities and nonprofits, once joked that he didn't suffer from attention deficit disorder (ADD) but from "attention abundance disorder (AAD)." He didn't lack curiosity, he said. His problem was that he wanted to rein in his curiosity and focus on fewer ideas. He's not alone. I imagine curiosity often stepping in to do wonder's bidding. First, wonder steps back and takes notice. It gets curiosity's attention and says, "Psst. Look at this. What's possible here?" Then curiosity takes off on a wild pursuit to learn more. After a while, curiosity dashes back home and empties its pockets of found objects and bits of knowledge on wonder's table.

You can see, then, how wonder can be considered to be the motor of human learning. Wonder precedes curiosity and starts this glorious process of gaining new knowledge and experience well into our grown-up years. The educational consultant Catherine L'Ecuyer agrees. In her article "The Wonder Approach to Learning" published in *Frontiers in Human Neuroscience*, she writes, "Wonder is what makes life genuinely personal." Without desire, meaning, and beauty, "the rigid and mechanical process of so-called learning through mere repetition becomes a deadening and alienating routine." Much of what we have accomplished at my Tracking Wonder consultancy is to bring a sense of wonder to how adult entrepreneurs and creative professionals *learn*. We have done so not only by creating rigorous training curricula in areas of creative flow and branding but also by creating experiences that elicit personal drive, collaboration, problem-tracking, and learning by doing.

If you've been on a creative exploration, you know the rush of discovery. You feel alive and lit up. Perhaps you cannot sleep at night, *not* because you're worried about the future but because you cannot wait for the next morning to map your discoveries—that conversion of a closet into a nook, that community garden project, that new event you yearn to host. The potentially nerve-racking piece of this experience is you have no idea what will come of your discoveries. Will your idea flop? Will your idea be worth it? But those questions don't stop you. They fuel you.

Evolutionary theorists posit that this distinctly human trait to pursue discovery developed to help us adapt at an unrivaled pace. It's encouraged by the particular neurochemical reaction of information seeking. Dopamine is the curiosity neurotransmitter, a chemical that sends signals between the brain's nerve cells, or neurons. Research shows that when our curiosity is piqued, dopamine rushes through the brain, which triggers the reward system and thus encourages us to dig deeper into our pursuits. It turns out that your brain in love—and your brain on good chocolate—is not unlike your brain in discovery mode, at least when it comes to the release of dopamine.

THE REBEL FACET

It's important to remember, though, that some of us have inherited cultural messages that can bias us against curiosity. Some of our most ancient stories about curiosity are threatening. Think of the consequences of Judaism's and Christianity's Adam and Eve, whose curiosity about the apple of knowledge gets them banished from Eden. The ever-curious Greek woman Pandora basically condemns humanity to a battle between good and evil by opening up that fateful box. Augustine of Hippo wrote that "God fashioned hell for the inquisitive." Yikes. Although many natural philosophers of the Enlightenment era favored a near-obsessive curiosity and meditation upon natural objects, many theologians deemed excessive curiosity as a distraction from faith. In one sense, I believe the modern-day cautionary tale about curiosity is to beware of its excess. Too much unfiltered curiosity—like that of my client "afflicted" with attention abundance disorder—can drive you to distraction.

But there's also another likely reason that figures of authority shut down other people's curiosity. Curiosity can be inherently subversive. It will not observe the rules. Curiosity questions everything. It loves to overturn orthodoxy, inquire into convention, and deviate from the normal route. Anyone wielding curiosity for a bit of time will naturally run up against authority. Just ask any innovator, from Darwin to Susan B. Anthony to Martin Luther King Jr. to Spanx founder Sara Blakely. Curiosity is the rebel facet.

Large segments of our culture are in the midst of a gradual transition from rule-bound convention to creative progress, and we are increasingly understanding how widespread curiosity helps advance our human endeavors for the better. Embracing curiosity in part has ushered in the largest wave of new ideas and technological innovation that we've ever witnessed.

But what keeps you going after the initial novelty hit? An active curiosity, it turns out, also could be a key facet in your persisting through creative and professional challenges.

KEEP QUESTING TO LEARN AGAIN—AND AGAIN

A few years ago, a woman posted a video on her blog to explain why she was tearing up her art—mostly random swirls of paint on small pieces of paper. Without a trace of irony, she said she had been "at it"—this artistic process she had made up for herself—off and on for a little over two years. She explained how as an untrained artist, she had taken an online course on selling her art, that she had given two years of her heart and soul to her own process, how she earnestly had tried to sell her swirls, but the response to buying her art was, in her words, "abysmal." She couldn't carry on, she said. She had made a dramatic decision: she was cutting up her soul-drenched work of the past two years. She then held up the swirls, one by one, and tore them up. Several people responded on the social media channel with sympathy and platitudes of encouragement. I had a different response. That episode seems like a sign of our times.

To put it plainly, in this time of false promises of "hacking mastery and success," there's a gap causing a lot of unspoken shame, confusion, and frustration. The gap in part has to do with false expectations of quick outward success leading to inner fulfillment. When these expectations aren't met, people blame themselves or "the marketplace." Maybe this young artist would have benefited from responding to her own responses with less dream-defeating self-judgment and more curious questions: "Why do I expect success? Have I asked other people for honest feedback about how I can improve my work? Why do I believe that the creative path is easy?" Her lack of curious experimentation with her creative process, it seemed, led her to go only in one swirly direction.

In fact, this amateur artist might have fallen prey to the "just follow your passion" myth, the idea that if you simply follow your passion, fulfillment will come. A series of studies out of Yale and Stanford concluded that people who held fast to this popular idea that following your passion leads to fulfillment ended up being less satisfied than people who instead followed their diverse curiosities. These diverse curiosities likely broadened their ability to handle disappointments and challenges. The curious people assumed more of what Carol Dweck, one of the study's psychologists, calls a "growth mindset." People with a growth mindset understand that they will need to pivot and reorient their direction as many times as are needed. They find fulfillment in the learning process as much as in the reward.

Their findings corroborate what happens in the brain. Colin G. DeYoung, who heads up the DeYoung Personality Lab at the University of Minnesota, calls dopamine the "neuromodulator of exploration" because it's released not just in receiving a reward but also *in pursuing it*. Its release helps us persist on the path of discovery despite inevitable uncertainty. When we're wonderstruck, the pleasure of the pursuit itself can be a worthwhile payoff.

I am fortunate to engage many accomplished professionals who have worked hard, delivered on their promises, and earned a living with a solid reputation. Yet they often come carrying an unspoken vulnerability and even shame. Shame because in this rapidly changing world, they think they "should" know what they don't know in order to produce their desired assets and projects— or they "should" be able to learn quickly and efficiently.

There is no shame in not knowing what you don't know. There is no shame in passing age thirty, or forty, or even seventy and still wanting and needing to learn new skills. This moment when you venture beyond your comfort zone is your opportunity to take each day's quest as another test of your wits and presence. Take stock of a set of skills you want to get better at and learn again to love to learn. Make your days part of a quest.

YOUNG GENIUS STORY

SRINI PILLAY

neuroscientist, founder of NeuroBusiness Group, poet, musician, and author of *Tinker, Dabble, Doodle, Try*

I grew up during apartheid in South Africa, though my family was originally from India. I remember walking on the "white" beach, where we were allowed to walk near the "white" pools, and I remember asking my mother if I could go into the pool, because I was a fairly fair-skinned child. And she said, "No. I'm sorry, darling, you can't go. It's for white people." And I said, "But I'm white." And she said, "Yes, but not white enough." At that moment, a single drop of the water left the pool and landed on my skin. I think that was a metaphor for what that whole experience was like for me. Because the excitement of being able to experience something that felt forbidden in that way, and the ability to sort of be aroused by that separateness, engaged by it, disappointed by it, I think sort of created a lot of different emotions. I grew up with a sense of love and interest and a sense of curiosity, rather than what a lot of people expect me to say, which is that growing up under these conditions was some kind of burden. Because even though the burden was there, I think that my curiosity lightened my load.

FOLLOW YOUR QUIRK

Wonder helps you take stock of what you, and possibly only you, are curious about. Consider the young genius of Oliver Sacks, the neurologist and historian of science who authored many best-selling books, including *Awakenings*, which was adapted to a successful film. In some of his last writings written as he knew he was dying, Sacks reflected on visiting London's Science Museum as a boy and seeing the periodic table for the first time. The elegant numerical chart of all the chemical combinations that make up this material world was sprawled across a giant wall. Standing there amid its aura, Sacks wrote that he felt "an overwhelming sense of Truth and Beauty," for he was certain that "these were indeed the elemental building blocks of the universe, that the whole universe was here, in microcosm, in South Kensington."

That moment must have lit up Sacks's young genius and set him on the trail of lifelong curiosity and a sense of wonder about existence. Once called "the poet laureate of medicine," Sacks would pursue his curiosity to shed light on little-understood neurological conditions such as autism, Tourette's syndrome, and musicophilia, improving the lives of patients and enlightening his reader audience of millions.

Your curiosities might not lead to scientific theories or insights, but your quirky inquisitiveness can advance you toward more creative fulfillment, even when outcomes are uncertain. All of us have peculiar interests, but there is a seminal advantage that innovators and everyday geniuses of creativity share: They honor and pay attention to them. They capture, track, and pursue those curiosities even if some of them send the innovator down tunnels or into the woods of their own imagination.

> **Your curiosities might not lead to scientific theories or insights, but your quirky inquisitiveness can advance you toward more creative fulfillment, even when outcomes are uncertain.**

Let's say you had the choice to pursue your idea for a safe life-coaching business or an as-of-yet undefined project related to (hear me out here) your questions about how dragonflies hover and navigate like helicopters. Play it safe and you might stick to life coaching. Play it curious, and you'll allow time on the side to track your quirks about, say, milky owlflies (a similar insect). After all, if you don't pursue your quirky curiosities, who will?

SLOW DOWN, PROVOKE PAUSE, AND BE RUNG

"Want to go hunt for leaves?" I asked our younger daughter, age six at the time. "*Shua*," she said, omitting the r sound in her adorable way as she grabbed two willow baskets to carry the goods. On a late September afternoon during one of my at-home workdays, the lush summer green foliage had started to change into a few hues of gold and crimson. Off we went. A few minutes into the woods, I realized that for much of the walk I had not seen much. My basket was empty, but my mind was full. I had limited time to get back to the studio to ensure I was sufficiently prepared for my next client meeting. I was, as we all get, distracted from the present. Several yards behind me, Alethea, squatting to the earth, surveyed a leaf in her hand. I resisted my forward trajectory and walked back to her.

"This one," she said, "has both green and red stripes." She held it up close to her eyes. "It's like it dropped to the ground before the red paint could finish. Or maybe the red is the leaf's blood coming out." I stooped down next to her. She handed it to me, and I tried to imagine the leaf once pulsing with a heartbeat and pumping veins. I wanted to slow down enough to experience what I had invited her to experience, but the pressure of time slipping away suddenly hoisted me up.

"I'm sorry, honey, but I must get back soon for my next meeting." She smiled and nodded, content, it seemed, with her handful of gold and red and mixed-colored treasures. One part of being a father, I have realized, is to ask for forgiveness over and over.

My daughter's pace reminded me that to pay attention to curiosity's hunches sometimes requires us to slow down. "When an idea or nudge grabs my attention," Barb Buckner Suárez told me, "I sit with it for a few days, maybe a week." Buckner Suárez is a valued member of my yearlong Inner Circle MasterMind group, a select group of business owners and thought leaders who are dedicated to tracking facets of wonder while advancing their endeavors with integrity. Buckner Suárez, a mother of four children, is a health educator and fellow of the Academy of Certified Childbirth Educators. She has taught thousands of families how to experience childbirth as a wondrous moment. One of the world's biggest athletic companies tapped her as a content expert for an app they created for pregnant women.

Ever curious and always learning, Buckner Suárez says she will "talk out an idea in the shower every morning. I think about how I would discuss it in an interview. Sometimes I share it with my husband or with people I'm working with to see how it lands. I write the first draft of what comes to me in one sitting and then I edit the crap out of it, twenty to twenty-five times! Then, once I hit publish, or turn the idea into a social media post, or create the presentation and send it to the conference coordinator, I kiss it goodbye and wait for the next inspiration!" Barb's avid inner explorations are matched by her outer ones: "I've gone skydiving, climbed a mountain, rode Class 4 rapids, and raced along a half-mile zip line above the Costa Rican rain forest at about fifty miles per hour," she writes on her website, "but none of that compares to how awesome birth is!" Buckner Suárez explodes every day.

But for others of us, curiosity often appears in a subtler, more interior manner. For me, it comes in the form of a vague hunch I have for a subject to pursue in a poem, project, or endeavor. I feel these inklings near dawn, before I fully wake up. You might have experienced such a moment when, as everything around and within you is enveloped in quiet, you sense an impulse, an image, a melody, or a word in your mind. It's remote, like a soft bell ringing in a forest. In your imagination, you follow it steadily and slowly to keep sensing the exact direction of the sound or feeling within.

I once pursued one of these ringing bells, making a list of words that seemed to have an undercurrent of similarity: *dissolve*, *evanescent, temporary, fleeting, transient, ephemeral.* That list is turning into my private "Lexicon of Vanishing." I'm tracking, I realized, my longtime fixation on the quicksilver passage of time, my sorrow about this planet's disappearing species and languages, and my melancholy toward mortality. These are all truths that heighten my wonder. That quirky obsession drives me to try to bear witness to time's passage.

Okay, pause here. I could list what these curiosities have led to (the writings and even Tracking Wonder's first product—that helps creative-minded people shape instead of manage time). Yet what I want to say is this: Sometimes you simply need to pursue your quirky curiosity because your genius force of character calls you to. Your curiosity doesn't always have to be productive. Sometimes it just wants to play *without why.*

To do so, sometimes you must provoke pause. Disrupt the default rapid pace of your day and your thinking. Listen. You need not expect to trace the source of the distant dawn ringing to a robed monk inviting you to sit on a cushion or a bejeweled goddess welcoming you to a feast. That is, don't pursue these hunches because you expect some grand insight. Follow them to see what you are indeed curious about. Sometimes, after following your curiosity, you realize *you* are the one being rung awake.

But fair warning: there are times when rebellious curiosity can draw us out toward something greater, that calls us to live difficult-to-answer questions.

CRACK OPEN WITH "WHAT IF?" AND FICTION

Asking questions is a way of being in the world.

ALAN LIGHTMAN

Travel to an island sanctuary off the coast of Maine and you might spy the theoretical astrophysicist, novelist, and self-described spiritual atheist Alan Lightman. Lightman is most renowned for his debut novel *Einstein's Dreams* published in 1993 while he was a professor of science, a professor of writing, and a senior lecturer in physics at Massachusetts Institute of Technology—the only professor there teaching both science and humanities. Yet this mind of such prominence doesn't identify with living in an ivory tower of answers. *Einstein's Dreams* is an innovative, lyrical, and plotless book composed of brief chapters, each of which is a fictional thought experiment: What if time went backward in a village? How would people live if, at the center of a village, time quickened and slowed down on its outskirts? The novel tested what a novel could be and do. Critics and readers alike applauded it, and it became an international bestseller. "Asking questions about the world is an active way of being in the world," Lightman said in an interview with *Poets & Writers*. "It's life for me, it's living."

Questioning *is* living for exemplary and everyday geniuses of creativity whose curiosities make a difference. They take their questions seriously, as outlandish, naive, or quirky as they may seem to friends or colleagues. Questioning enlivens us and opens us up. Then a recursive cycle begins. Our curiosity can prompt fruitful questions, and those questions in turn can feed our curiosity—not only to find answers but also to experiment with possible solutions. The right *kinds* of questions framed well can shape the experimental action you take in advancing your endeavor.

If you watched the Academy Awards in 2001, you probably wouldn't have been thinking at all about the longevity of the glamorous people accepting trophies on the gilded stage. Most of us would have just been dazzled at the spectacle and happy for the winners. Yet the scientist and medical doctor Donald A. Redelmeier had some different thoughts that night as he watched Julia Roberts win best actress and Russell Crowe win best actor. He noticed how much more vivaciously their bodies moved than, say, his own patients. That observation launched a series of intuitive questions: Is there a correlation between success and longevity? Between public recognition and longevity? *How* could that correlation be tested? Dr. Redelmeier put his hunch into action and devised a study in which he determined the age of death of every Academy Award winner and the runners-up. The finding: winners outlive the runners-up by almost four years.

After he published this study, the *New York Times* called Dr. Redelmeier "perhaps the leading debunker of preconceived notions in the medical world." In the 1980s, when Redelmeier finished medical training at a California hospital, he noticed something else. On Super Bowl Sundays, the hospital became inundated with accident victims. So fifteen years later, he followed a hunch, researched statistics, and concluded that on Super Bowl Sundays, there's a 41 percent relative increase in fatalities because of drunk driving. Furthermore, he was first on the scene to study the correlation between cell phone use and car accidents. His 1997 study concluded that people who drive while using cell phones are four times more likely to have an automobile accident than drivers who do not.

Redelmeier, an acknowledged master in his field, stays fresh by maintaining an agile experimenter's questioning attitude. This attitude helps him further his pursuit of knowledge while not succumbing to know-it-all syndrome. In fact, his disruptive and innovative questions might have the effect of humbling his peers, too, nudging them to investigate their hunches, even if they are way out of the normal line of investigation. The Super Bowl, the Academy Awards—anything can be possible fodder for the curious rebel's trail of questions.

Redelmeier doesn't fear asking what would appear to be "dumb" questions. He also doesn't fear his colleagues' criticism. In 2005, he spoke at an *Annals of Internal Medicine* conference that examined issues related to medical errors. Dr. Redelmeier applied four heuristics, or patterns of thinking, from cognitive psychology that might illuminate why doctors misdiagnose patients. In a follow-up interview with cardiologist Lee Goldman, then of the University of California, San Francisco, Redelmeier acknowledged that these mental constructs likely cannot be avoided. "What can be beaten out of us [doctors], though," he said, "is this enormous sense of arrogance."

If you've ever been met by an incurious doctor, you know how important Redelmeier's mission is. Redelmeier's heuristics have an ambitious aim for doctors during the critical diagnosis stage: to keep their minds open and not succumb too quickly to what psychologists call a need for cognitive closure (NFC). NFC is almost counter to the very state of mind we're describing as optimal— it's our aversion to ambiguity and desire for certainty. There is nothing inherently wrong or flawed with this attribute of human cognition, but a high need for closure correlates with drops in creativity and rationality. Do you often leap to the quick, easy, and safe answer? Do you over-rely on one way to solve a problem—especially if you've met with success in the past by using that method? It's okay. We all do. But we don't all notice ourselves doing it. That's the key to creating a new perspective.

Keith Oatley tracks these cognitive biases and how to bust them. He is a professor emeritus of cognitive psychology at the University of Toronto and a novelist, which might explain his fascination with the role that reading fiction plays in opening our minds. In the 2013 study "Opening the Closed Mind: The Effect of Exposure to Literature on the Need for Closure," Oatley and two colleagues concluded that exposure to literary short stories with ambiguous endings—versus essays—keeps readers' minds open. The implications, they noted, could be useful when considering how doctors make diagnoses. Doctors might need more exposure to ambiguity to keep their minds open to unconventional answers.

But what are the implications for you? To generate more questions than answers in your mind, try reading or listening to short stories (if you don't have time to read a novel). Why? Further studies by Oatley and other scientists show that when you immerse yourself in reading fiction, you stimulate your imagination—the very faculty that allows you to conceive new ideas, make strange combinations, and invent new worlds. Many fictional stories explore greater truths by beginning with a "What if?" premise, such as Lightman's *Einstein's Dreams*. What would happen if time stood still in the center of a village? If you prime your mind in the morning with a question like this, then a coworker's stray comment or something you read from a *National Geographic* article over lunch could spark a new connection to your own question. By reminding yourself of your queries, you're priming your mind for serendipity via curiosity.

Questions that begin with "What if?" and "Why not?" naturally crack us open to possibility.

Here are some examples that might come from your personal curiosity:

What if our family went out one night a week to do something new?

Why couldn't I learn to play mandolin?

Here are some examples of powerful questions that led to discoveries:

"What if women—especially, but not only busy mothers—practiced the art of deep rest every day?" which led to "What if rested women told stories of reclaiming their power and this changed the dominant cultural narrative?" (Karen Brody, author of *Daring to Rest* and founder of the yoga nidra movement of the same name)

"What if an alarm clock rolled off the nightstand so you couldn't hit the snooze button?" (Gauri Nanda, founder of Clocky)

If you have a business with team meetings, the next time your team meets to consider a new initiative, invite the ever-curious (if not slightly rebellious) team members to listen and raise intelligently naive questions. This is what you might hear:

> Why can't we create a business model that centers on time off work?

> What if we started hosting open community workshops at our auto mechanic garage?

> What if our schools were designed to foster everyone's diverse talents instead of just the academically capable?

When you live in questions that matter to you, a day becomes part of a quest of serendipity instead of a quagmire of to-dos.

EXPERIMENT LIKE A SCIENTIST

Approach everything you pursue hypothetically and bravely test your assumptions. Get messy and enjoy the discoveries. And above all else, embrace experimenting over perfectionism and over-planning. Conducting little experiments with your endeavors reframes your work as part scientific method, part creative process, and—if relevant to you—part entrepreneurial risk-taking. To experiment like a scientist invites you to take incremental steps with what the author Peter Sims calls "little bets"—small, low-risk actions to discover, develop, and test an idea. If you want to repaint your whole house, start by painting a bathroom and see what you learn works and doesn't. If you want to lead a new kind of workshop but you've never led a workshop before, invite three friends and three of their friends to your house, and test it out on them. What's essential is to get curious both about your process and about the results. Ask yourself a set of questions to prod your curiosity. "What did I learn that works in the process? What were the results? What didn't turn out the way I assumed? Why not? Where did I derive fulfillment both in the process and the results?" That kind of reflection helps you make more meaning of your activities and assess best next steps.

But, you know, every curious wonder tracker needs a physical space to capture and gather curiosities.

MAKE A CURIOSITY
CABINET OR CORNER

Our dreams, quirks, and hunches are not always visible. That can be a problem if your life is full and your attention is divided daily. Those early morning hunches can slip down the shower drain of forgetfulness. How can you playfully collect your curiosities so they become a reminder of the trails you want to pursue? You could test out creating a curiosity cabinet or curiosity corner.

In sixteenth-century Europe, it became a practice among educated and passionate collectors to create cabinets of curiosities (*kunstkammers*) and cabinets of wonder (*wunderkammers*). Sometimes these weren't just singular displays but entire rooms full of exultant wonders gathered from various explorations—original illustrations, owl eggs, whale bones, peacock feathers, exotic beetles, rare stamps, shells, or microsculptures. Many curiosity cabinets were designed to instill a sense of mystery, even a kind of *trembling awe* about what you don't know.

Stephen Greenblatt describes this era in his book *Marvelous Possessions: The Wonder of the New World*. Wonder was the central European response to the New World explorations; it was the decisive emotional and intellectual experience *in the presence of radical difference*. "Columbus's voyage initiated a century of intense wonder," he writes, not unlike an infant's startle reflex of widened eyes and stilled breath. Wonder cabinets reflect the drive to know and the indisputable facts of what you do not know. Maybe you didn't believe the sailor's tales, but how could you deny the fascinating (narwhal) horn before your eyes that was rumored to have dropped from a unicorn?

Charles Darwin, for instance, had an abiding quirky curiosity about—yep—earthworms, and he had a designated space in his basement to honor this fascination. For several years, he grappled with his theories of evolution and natural selection, and how to present them not only in scientific circles and publications but also eventually in cogent book-length arguments. His basement acted as a brave laboratory, another kind of curiosity cabinet. He played the piano to record how the earthworms responded to sound and tracked their preferences for being fed cabbage or mint. In his last published book, *The Formation of Vegetable Mould, Through the Action of Worms, with Observations on Their Habits,* he showed that the underground dwellers are not simply garden pests but also the singular force responsible for arable soil. I imagine that in times of trouble and uncertainty, as Darwin battled health problems, professional insecurity, and church authoritarianism, his evenings with the worms must have provided him with a stable source of curiosity.

One of my clients, Brandy Donovan, an emerging portrait photographer, lives outside of San Diego with her three young children and engineer husband. She decided one summer that it was time for the family to emphasize their creativity together. She covered a wall with her husband's oversized engineering plan paper and called it a "Wonder Wall." Each time a family member wondered about something, they headed to the Wonder Wall to write or draw a picture of what they were wondering about. Her eight-year-old son wrote that he wondered if computers and robots know everything in the universe, since he noticed that he could ask Siri (the iPhone artificial intelligence app) anything. Spurred on by this question, she and her son had a conversation about whether computers can know everything.

BRANDY:
I think that anything is possible, though I know that as of today, computers don't know love; they don't know how we're feeling, nor do they know how to have a meaningful conversation.

SON:
What about *Tracking Wonder* or Krista Oprah? (Note: Brandy's son apparently listens to our podcast, along with Oprah Winfrey's *Super Soul and Krista Tippett's On Being* podcast, with Brandy. In his child's mind, the two hosts are one—"Krista Oprah.") Those seem like meaningful talks, but they come to us on a computer.

BRANDY:
Yes, they are meaningful, but the computer is simply the tool bringing something meaningful from one soul to another, not the meaning itself.

Brandy went on to say that "experimenting with wonder is so simple but so transformative! Wonder and curiosity now inform our daily schedule."

The truth is that a wide-eyed openness and subversive curiosity also can inform your days at home, at work, and in the creative studio. If you track them more consistently, I could almost promise that the clouds above you will start to assume shapes of rockets and superheroes again, and the horizon you gaze toward will lead you and the people you affect toward a better place of possibility.

Why not approach each day that way?

CURIOSITY

Make Each Day a Quest

Begin here if you feel that you've neglected your curiosity.
Cultivate a curiosity habit to make every day a quest of discovery.
In this way, your life is not bifurcated between something that
lights you up and "the other stuff" you must tend to on any
given day. "Create in integrity, not in battle," we often say at
Tracking Wonder. Your day might become a flow in which your
curiosities gain traction from your increased self-motivating
questioning *and reflection*. Each morning reflect on one or
more of these prompts in your Tracking Wonder notebook:

Today I am curious about_____.
How might my experiences today inform
what I am curious about and vice versa?

What do I not know about _____?
What challenge (a decision or task)
am I likely to face today?

How can my young genius traits
and other strengths and skills come
forward to finesse that challenge?
What discovery would excite
me to pursue today?

And take it a step further. Live in a hard-to-answer "What
if?" or "Why not?" question of your own. Soak in the question and see if you don't feel just a bit cracked open to
what's possible in this one life.

At the very least, begin with that first prompt: "Today I am curious about_____." For instance, let's say there's a personal problem or professional challenge bothering you. You might avoid it, over-worry about it, hope someone else or the Universe will deal with it, or just wish it away. An alternative approach, though, is to bring your curiosity forward and make your day more questful. Take a moment to train your attention on that specific challenge or problem that you'd like insight into. Get curious about it. Remember, you have the power to change the quality of your days. Get curious and questful.

Be Rung with What You Care About

If you tend to be introspective and if your curiosity shows up in subtler ways, try this invitation. Have your Tracking Wonder notebook nearby.

CENTER. Find a quiet place at a time of day when there are few distractions around you. Bring your attention to your breath.

ASK YOURSELF, "WHAT HAVE I BEEN CURIOUS ABOUT FOR A LONG TIME?" "What do I want to investigate?" Listen to your inner voice. What's "ringing" within you? Sometimes one or more words will float past your attention like candidates in a contest. Sometimes an image will surface.

WRITE DOWN OR DRAW WHATEVER GETS YOUR ATTENTION, BUT DO SO SLOWLY. Do it as if each line you're writing or sketching were a step closer to a bell ringing from a forest that calls you out of your living room or office. Tend to where a word or line might take you. The aim here is to let slow writing or slow drawing help you follow your internal signals as to what you and only you might be curious about.

Connect Your Curiosity to What You Care About

This next invitation helps you take the previous one a step further and may take a few days to do properly. But it's helpful if you feel as if your curiosity often runs amok. In an interview with the Academy-nominated filmmaker Mark Osborne (*Kung Fu Panda*, *The Little Prince*), Osborne told me that what got his team through the travails of every film was that they each found a deep and personal connection to the film project. Wonder keeps asking curiosity to pause, reflect, and care.

CONNECT YOUR CURIOSITY TO WHAT YOU CARE ABOUT. Say you're excited about cooking and have always wanted to expand your repertoire. You might decide to work your way through a cookbook about Japanese cooking. Or say you have always wanted to help injured wildlife in your area, since there is no facility providing that service. What questions are you called to get answered to start doing that important work? Devote consistent attention to making something you deeply care about or to making a new solution for something you care about.

FURTHER EXPLORE YOUR MISSION. Now, after starting this curiosity quest, you can sit somewhere relatively free from distractions to align yourself with this mission. Take a moment to be quiet. For the next four mornings, in your Tracking Wonder notebook, explore your responses to one or more of these questions. You can respond by writing, sketching, or doodling:

Why am I creating what I am creating? Why do I care?

What personal story connects me to the heart of what I am creating?

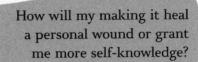

How will my making it heal
a personal wound or grant
me more self-knowledge?

What new knowledge do
I want to pursue, research,
or acquire?

By making it, what skills could
I get to learn or hone?

What resources and people outside
of my knowledge could I seek out?

Create a Personal or Professional Curiosity Cabinet

When you were a child, did you fill your pockets with bottle caps, pieces of plastic, and simple stones for whatever world you were making? I did. And I still do. I've just replaced the bottle caps with articles, photos, and index cards.

Try this invitation to enhance your physical environment and keep cueing your imagination. A personal or professional curiosity cabinet might be a table, a shelf, an actual cabinet, or a corner of a space devoted to your curiosities and creative endeavors. Several clients include a large flip-chart-sized sheet of poster board that keeps track of their ideas and insights on color-coded sticky notes. Their curiosity corners look sort of like those walls you see in thriller films in which an ever-curious detective is trying to see patterns and connect dots among disparate facts and data. Brandy's Wonder Wall was also a great way to engage this exercise.

What's included in *your* "cabinet" space or curiosity corner?

Try setting up books, print articles, photographs, magazine images, sketches, notebooks, musical instruments—in short, anything you *select* that, daily, reminds your curious, creative mind about what matters. A blank whiteboard that you'll fill with your questions can be a great memento of curiosity. Or maybe you'll take a cue from the curiosity cabinet curators and bring in all the natural objects that strike your fancy: a pine cone altar, a feather mandala, or a mini zen garden of lichen-crusted stones.

Even a tray can do the trick. Shari Daniels, who reads and follows my work, describes herself on one of her social media profiles as a "possibilitarian" and "learner and forever curious." How appropriate, then, that she posted her experience in learning how to provoke pause amid her productive waves and take short wonder walks. She returns with bounty on her curiosity tray—a simple tray that reads "Let Life Surprise You," on which she places found objects that spark her curiosity: rocks, feathers, dried burdock.

Your mind will ultimately become your portable curiosity cabinet, and your collection of questions and quests will make a big difference in your lived experience.

CHAPTER 6

BEWILDERMENT, THE DEEP WOODS FACET

LOST IN THE MIDDLE

ONE DAY, IN THE early phase of building Tracking Wonder as a business, I went to the woods to get lost deliberately. Sort of. After taking care of our newborn daughter for most of the morning, I had spent much of the afternoon fulfilling obligations to new clients and hires, tasking the ticking minutes with keyboard-tapping fingers and a rattling mind. Once my wife could take over duties, near dusk, I found myself called to roam the woods and meadows behind our house. Among the birch and pine, the red-winged blackbirds and catbirds, I had been ruminating on how off-center I felt in ways I couldn't clearly define. I had been trying to merge my roles as a provider (father, husband, business owner) and my work as a poet (writer, teacher, and creator). In a simplistic way, these selves felt at odds. The dutiful provider roles wouldn't quite reconcile with the more exploratory poet roles. Would I ever meet my own high expectations?

While lost in thought, suddenly a sound I had never heard before stopped me in the woods. *Who-cooks-for-you.* Pause. Again. *Who-cooks-for-you* and then, a rolling chortle. I paused, looked around, and realized I had lost my bearings. I knew I was in no danger. The woods weren't vast. No search squads would be called. Yet with a jolt of adrenaline and quickened heartbeat, my surroundings came into vivid relief—the fuzzy green lichen on stones, a catbird's scratchy song, the faint red poison oak strands that roped around a black walnut. The act of being fairly disoriented heightened my awareness as if I had super senses. "Why was that?" I later wondered. "Why, when lost, can our senses and cognition wake us up in full spectrum?"

I would later identify those unfamiliar sounds as a pair of barred owls who continue to inhabit these woods—and their call still enchants me. The thing is, though, I was less intrigued by the surprise and more curious about my response to the surprise. During that period of parental and professional role definition, I continued to take these walks, often deliberately trying to get lost. These bewildering walks paradoxically gave me direction while I held space for the confusing battle inside me. It would take quite a while before I rewove those emerging and existing selves in a way that allowed me to feel free. How I did so is a part of this chapter.

The truth is, I'm comfortable with high degrees of cognitive and existential confusion. I find the world fascinating and puzzling, worthy of ongoing questions: "Who am I? What do I have to contribute? How can our species evolve to live together better—more creatively and less reactively?" Since my thirties, I have worked with people who go through long stages of confusion. The melee in their businesses and endeavors inevitably overlaps with uncertainty about their identities. Many of them have been profoundly uncomfortable with this uncertainty and yet they still have hungered for a way to pass through the unknown territory, sensing some greater possibility "on the other side."

Something clicked. When I looked not only to the innovators I had studied but also to the psychology of creativity and personal growth, I corroborated a key hunch about emergent roles: I wanted to help them navigate, if not celebrate, this stage of becoming. I then started seeking more deliberate questions about bewilderment and confusion: "What are these states? Why do we deny them? And how could they become a more fruitful frame of mind?"

Both everyday and exemplary geniuses of creativity, it turns out, learn to welcome these periods for gradual personal and professional breakthrough. But it often requires a detour into uncomfortable uncertainty, which is the facet of wonder I call bewilderment.

FACET 3: BEWILDERMENT

Bewilderment is the disorienting facet of wonder. The verb *bewilder* means "to cause (someone) to become perplexed and confused." *Bewilderment* essentially means "to thoroughly go astray." But I also like to imagine bewilderment as the state to "be wilder." By that I mean that tracking this facet could be an invitation for you to explore other dormant parts of your life, work, and identity. It arises as a response to surprise when we're in profound transition by necessity, circumstance, calling, or all of those. When in bewilderment, you can feel at once exhilarated by the new world you might venture into while also feeling confused, if not lost. Isn't it paradoxical that one way to *find* deep fulfillment often requires getting temporarily *lost*? Perhaps more than any other facet of wonder, bewilderment can unhinge your comfortable sense of reality. (Yikes.) So why would you deliberately track this facet?

> **Isn't it paradoxical that one way to *find* deep fulfillment often requires getting temporarily *lost*?**

Bewilderment holds beautiful truths. It potentially challenges and thus enlarges our safe sense of self. The mystery of who we are and could become surfaces to our awareness, as if we were a child again. This kind of surprising phase might spark inaction and fear, or it could bring forward your young genius, intelligent naiveté, and curiosity in new contexts.

So much is possible.

Yes, bewilderment is a space rife with possibility, and you can learn to track it for your own personal and creative breakthroughs.

FEEL THE CONFUSION

By the time Tracy Fullerton was thirty-seven, she had become surprisingly successful in the speculative digital world of the 1990s. As a woman, Fullerton was a pioneer by leading in a male-dominated space. Founder and president of a startup, Spiderdance, Inc., Fullerton was renowned for offering pioneering interactive television programming for MTV, NBC, and the History Channel—work that earned her an Emmy nomination for interactive television. She told her story on the *Tracking Wonder* podcast. Fullerton's internet-based future looked bright on the cusp of the millennium, but then the dot-com bubble burst and so did Fullerton's business.

Something else popped open for Fullerton in this unexpected setback: her sense of who she was, what was real, and what was meaningful work. After all, her work in the digital world had been building so quickly that she had not paused long enough to entertain bigger questions about her purpose and her gifts to the world. At the time, many of her peers sought comfort in rapidly finding other jobs or just numbing out. She could've done likewise. Instead, as discomforting as it was, she took an extended break to reflect on where she had been with her life and where she might go. She chose to *feel* the confusion. She didn't run away from it.

I've worked with many people like Fullerton who've changed career courses or advanced their grand endeavors in comparable ways. When I ask people to describe how they feel in these unsettling situations, they often use words such as *floating*, *dizzy*, or *free-falling*. Remember in the film version of *The Wizard of Oz*, a tornado lifts Dorothy from a Kansas farm—her land of familiar comfort—as she literally spins in her tornado moment and lands in Oz. A few minutes after stepping into this Technicolor reality, she utters her famous line, "Toto, I've a feeling we're not in Kansas anymore." At this moment, she has no idea what will befall her. She is bewildered. Yet she doesn't evince fear; she's a bit trepidatious, but also enraptured. Or think of Lewis Carroll's Alice, whose trip down the rabbit hole disorients her. In well-known literature, the realms such as Oz, Wonderland, and Narnia present bewildered characters the opportunity to redeem their best selves, solve problems, and become masterful participants in meaningful stories. But these moments are not just fictional opportunities.

Wonder often challenges the self-defined roles we play ("I am a teacher." "I am an accountant." "I am a Buddhist." "I am an environmental activist." "I am a CEO.") and "de-centers" the self. The cognitive neuroscientist Kelly Bulkeley noted that when we feel wonder, our "ordinary sense of personal identity is dramatically altered, leading to new knowledge and understanding that ultimately *recenters* the self." Wonder, benign as it may seem, does not always protect our well-constructed identity, unlike the emotions of disgust or humiliation that further entrench our ego. Wonder drops our guard, and our sense of self can be left vulnerable for reinvention as our rigid roles might dissolve or overlap.

We all have tornado moments. Imagine your own. What profoundly surprising situations seemingly beyond your control have spun you for a loop? How did you respond? Did you think you were to blame? Were you able to spin initial fear into fascination? How were you able to get your footing and move forward with your life goals, perhaps with a new perspective and renewed courage? Now, consider this: When you venture toward living this one life with more creativity and artful resilience, you likely will induce your own tornado moments.

As you stretch into terra incognito, you may, like an extended rubber band, want to contract to a familiar place. That's an understandable reaction. It can be helpful, though, to stop in your tracks and feel what you're feeling. Really, *feel the confusion* is an essential step to not bypass this experience. How does your moment of bewilderment feel in your body? Along your skin? What feelings come up for you? Are you nervous about letting go of anything? Do you feel as if a part of you is dying? This question is really important: In your personal tornado moment, what would you compare these feelings to—being adrift on the ocean or lost in wild woods? Are you curious about the unknown possibilities of what could be birthed and created? Acknowledge the tension. Doing so lets more of you accept this state as an opportunity for growth and discovery. Feel it. Don't flee it.

CELEBRATE THE CONFUSION

I am a fool, oh yes, I am confused.

LAO TZU

ancient Chinese sage and author of the Tao Te Ching

"I'm not who I used to be anymore, and I don't know who I'm becoming. And that feels amazing. As if for the first time in my life, anything is possible." That's what my client Carol told me. Sixty-three at the time, she had grown up on Long Island, and for over twenty years she had identified as a professor to struggling students, daughter to an ailing mother, mother to two troubled children, and wife to a distant husband. Those roles defined her. Why this new feeling of possibility? During the previous two years while we worked together, she had taken overseas trips to Scotland to conduct research and interviews for her first book, she had paid more attention to her photography, she had said no to course assignments that no longer served her fullest potential, and she had learned to monitor her emotions as a way to guide her own course of creative living. She started hosting local events that showcased her photography and the creative expression of friends and colleagues. People started to see her differently, and she saw herself differently. She had redefined her current roles as artist and writer while still maintaining her existing roles. Who was she becoming? She didn't know. Carol, like Alice in Wonderland, was in bewilderment. Many people bristle at not-knowing, yet a growing number of people like Carol are discovering what poets, artists, and mystics in the East and West have known for centuries: bewilderment can be a creative place to celebrate being in.

The world-renowned personal growth expert Tony Robbins harnesses this little-known bit of wisdom to help people develop a new type of helpful reaction to bewilderment. At his seminars attended by thousands of people seeking to improve their lives, he often calls on audience members to stand up and explain an issue they are grappling with. If anyone admits to being confused, Robbins encourages the crowd to give them a standing ovation. Robbins knows that uncertainty is the bridge between one level of understanding and the next, so he applauds their recognizing this pivotal state. But he's also doing something wise on a neurological and existential, if not spiritual, level. Robbins recognizes that these moments, when our deep constructs of identity and reality become challenged, are opportunities for true growth and learning.

Surprises are learning opportunities. Because our brains process novel information and sensory input and then file away memories in the same region, we actually pay more attention to and remember what surprises us. Psychologists have tested whether surprise amplifies learning by looking at how infants respond to various unexpected events. Aimee Stahl, a professor in the College of New Jersey's Department of Psychology, and Lisa Feigenson, the codirector of the John Hopkins University Laboratory for Child Development, conducted a series of experiments that deliberately defied infants' expectations. In some experiments, for instance, infants watched a ball appear to pass through a wall or through a screen. They already had the basic understanding that objects cannot move through opaque surfaces, so this event was surprising to view. The babies not only paid more attention to the object that surprised them, but the element of surprise also correlated with their increased learning about one of the object's properties.

The right amount of confusion deepens learning. The scientists concluded that when infants' expectations of core knowledge are defied, they learn better, explore more, and "test relevant hypotheses for that object's behavior." Their conclusions confirm René Descartes's observations in 1649 when he published the first modern detailed account of human emotions, *Les passions de l'ame* (*The Passions of the Soul*). He wrote that experiences of surprising wonder—even though often fleeting in duration—deepen our memory. If everyday experiences happen in lowercase, surprising ones are all caps and bold. They're the ones that stand out and give us more grounding to respond confidently. If we resist feelings of fear, cognitive dissonance, and confusion, we may miss the very opportunities that will help us flourish.

What is in this phase of being bewildered for you to learn? For confusion to have a profound impact on you, you must expend quite a bit of mental energy to suspend the urge to escape it. Our brains, after all, are wired for a fight-or-flight response that we have evolved to make rapid decisions key to our survival. Yet if you can trip your brain's hardwired response to dispatch the confusion not as a threat but as an opportunity, you can step further into the woods, so to speak, with more creativity than reactivity.

HOLD THE SPACE BETWEEN

To navigate bewilderment amid inevitable fears, we need boundaries and we need breathing. If gone unchecked, perpetual fear can trigger a negative cycle in the body. Many studies corroborate that anxiety arouses our body's sympathetic nervous system, which in turn can trigger shallow breathing or unconscious breath holding. The tricky thing is that unconsciously holding your breath can, in turn, arouse the body's fight-or-flight response and compound anxiety. This spiral complicates our ability to respond proactively and creatively. Yet the very hormonal chain reactions that create fear also induce excitement, and you can metabolize fearful reactivity into exciting creativity by using the power of your full breath.

Thanks to many studies conducted in the 1970s and '80s, we know that inhalations increase our heartbeat and exhalations slow down our heartbeat. In fact, slowing down your exhalation and even pausing for a nanosecond in that space between exhalation and inhalation can calm your sympathetic nervous system. That saying "Just breathe out" has validity in the body. If you want to transform the revved-up energy you feel into readiness to navigate the unknown, breathe deeply while also directing your thoughts to engage creatively with the experience.

YOUNG GENIUS STORY

TRACY FULLERTON
video game designer

At that age, the most magical place was my dad's workshop in the garage. My brothers and sisters and I were always going in there and making things, even though we weren't supposed to touch any of the tools! Of course we did anyway. We would wind up making all sorts of contraptions and clubhouses, or whatever we could think of or find parts for.

My dad was an engineer, and he did a lot of building around our house, so there were always a lot of tiny little pieces of electrical wires, or the things that pop out of electrical sockets that you could use to glue on and make your own spaceship, or whatever it was you were working on that day.

That imaginative play with whatever we could find in the garage set the stage for a lifetime of my creative work.

Think of it another way. Your physical symptoms that result from your body's fight-or-flight reaction are neutral. They are a biological reaction that prepares you to act quickly and with great energy. If you overreact with fear, anger, or anxiety, then that almond-shaped part of your hindbrain, the amygdala, acts like a startled guard to alert you to a three-alarm fire. It sets off the sympathetic nervous system's cortisol-infused chain reaction of stress. It takes a long time to get back to equilibrium. It takes repeated practice to recondition your response, so aim to practice breathing deeply with extended exhalations each time something surprising throws you off course, whether it's a frozen computer screen, a lost job, or a new diagnosis.

You can pause long enough to be more curious than distressed. Tracy Fullerton, rather than seeking another ready opportunity immediately, went to a place that had inspired her young genius as a girl on family vacations: Walden Pond. This was the spot outside of Boston where America's first renowned life designer, Henry David Thoreau, spent two epic years living in the peace and quiet of a solitary cabin. Thoreau had retreated to the woods to question things. He had recently suffered enormous losses, which led to his bewilderment. His beloved older brother had suddenly died of lockjaw, Thoreau's proposal to a woman he loved had been rejected, and he hadn't found success in conventional society, despite having a Harvard degree and the patronage of the prominent poet Ralph Waldo Emerson. So Thoreau built a cabin, conducted his own life experiment over eight seasons, and captured his discoveries and observations on the deliberately simple life in his masterpiece, *Walden*. Fullerton had always known that this book held wisdom about what really matters in our hustle-and-bustle world that still holds true nearly two centuries after its publication.

In a way, Fullerton's personal journey to Walden was her way to hold the space between the past and the future. Going to a familiar place while in a personally unfamiliar inner space gave her a safe boundary to explore. While Fullerton wandered the woods and sat among the birds and birch, she got the seed of a seemingly crazy, if not utterly paradoxical, idea: What if you could create video games that countered the typical adrenaline-producing, first-person shooter scenario with an adventure that instilled meaning, contemplation, and—yes—wonder? What if it could be done in such a way that contributed more value to our crazed culture at large than the harmful effects of many video games? What if that video game were based on one man's life who ventured into the woods and who questioned our ready reliance on technology? Those "What if?" questions lit her up. Do you see how she brought forward her young genius, her openness to possibility, and her What if? curious questioning? She lit up her wonder mind.

Think of your wonder mind—versus your downer mind—as the safe and brave container for your transformation. It's the incubator for creative bewilderment. Befriend your wonder mind in this pause. Whether or not you can "get away" to some other physical place, be curious about your confusion. Drawing from the facet of curiosity, phrase your own positive "What if?" questions that make you curious about this quest.

When you pause long enough to get curious, you suspend the stress response and your panicky amygdala calms down while your much more relaxed hippocampus lights up. This part of the brain detects novel information and sensory input. It's involved in decision-making, learning, and long-term memory. The hippocampus is also a key area where your adult brain can generate new neurons, which science has only recently confirmed. We used to think that brain cells were finite, but according to some studies, an adult hippocampus might generate seven hundred neurons a day. A healthy hippocampus can look like a healthy forest whose multiple tree branches spread and form multiple pathways (perhaps to get productively lost in!).

FERTILIZE CONFUSION

If you feel it, celebrate it, and get curious about it, then you can fertilize confusion. That's right: *fertilize* it. You fertilize confusion in part by directing your attention toward an activity or endeavor that demands your full-spectrum focus and creativity. Here's another bit of counterintuitive insight to help you understand why the state of bewilderment can work magic on you.

Remember the importance of the flow state? As Kelly McGonigal wrote in her book *The Upside of Stress*, top performers in all kinds of fields are not calm when they make art, play sports, or perform surgery. They are in a positive state of stress or activation that "gives them access to their mental and physical resources, and the result is increased confidence, enhanced concentration, and peak performance." If you can embrace the energy you feel and get more creatively focused than fearful, it will supercharge your performance and actually transform your underlying physiology.

Every big idea begets a series of challenges. I've been surprised by how many everyday geniuses of creativity I've worked with have learned to deal with surprise. Consistently they *learn to expect* challenges to arise in pursuing their endeavors. Most of these people weren't born with those expectations and mindset. They fostered a more successful approach by expecting surprises and preparing for them. We must be open and willing to leave our maps behind and accept our confusion if we want to become wiser.

I call this creative approach "fertile confusion" because we can use confusion to see ourselves anew and to redefine aspects of our lives or who we are through creative experiments. When you fertilize confusion, you can till the soil of your soul. Fertile confusion is a state in which you refrain from seeking easy solutions or reverting to old patterns long enough to transform your worldview, yourself, or your approach to a complex endeavor. Exemplary and everyday geniuses of creativity learn to welcome cognitive confusion as an invitation to challenge their assumptions, gather more knowledge, and test out ideas.

Tracy Fullerton's "What if" questions about converting *Walden* into a video game lit her up. But they were quickly followed by the breath-stopping question, "How?"—as in "How could I pull this off?" It would take Fullerton over a decade to find the answers to those questions she lived, but she gained traction in 2008 when she was named director of the USC Game Innovation Lab in Los Angeles. There she found a team of allies who would live these questions with her.

How would Fullerton keep nudging such a complex and countercultural project forward? How would they get funding? She figured out that she needed her team to get invested in the insights contained in the original source, Walden. "I had no money and no prospect of any money," Tracy told me, "because while you can pitch ideas obviously in the game industry and get funding, you can't pitch this idea." With several hardcover copies of Walden, she and interested team members started a personal book club. They regularly discussed which passages personally spoke to each of them. They eventually (five years later) landed their first funder, the National Endowment for the Arts, which gave them a grant that led to further funding by the National Endowment for the Humanities and the Sundance Institute. Persistence over a decade paid off. Ten years of development later, the result is a video game with a moving narrative, a contemplative pace befitting the subject, stunning visuals and auditory effects, and a depth of learning discoveries.

In the game, players practice the survival skills that Thoreau engaged in every day, using an avatar that stands in for him. They gather wood, fish in the pond, maintain his cabin, and tend to a garden. They learn about Thoreau's role in the Underground Railroad and Thoreau's advanced studies of herbalism, and they read passages from books that Thoreau and his mentor Emerson studied. As Thoreau the character gets exhausted from his hard-driving lifestyle, the world goes increasingly gray and he loses "inspiration," which can be regained if the players can find it in the surrounding woods. Every effort was made to make the environment immersive and engaging: birds chirp, wind rustles the leaves, shadows rise and fall realistically as the sun moves through the sky. Berry bushes flower and fruit, the pond freezes over and thaws, birds migrate, tools and clothing need mending. Contemplative and soothing, it is an extraordinarily different game experience that also teaches the tenets of transcendentalism, a philosophy that he, Emerson, and other thinkers were known for.

Again, remember that every big idea begets a series of challenges. Even with so much support, *Walden, a game* faced continuous problems—from funding to team morale to technical details. Yet Fullerton and her devoted team persisted by staying openly creative, curious, and collaborative in ways that fueled them forward.

You might not have a ready-made lab hosted by a renowned institution available to you, but I've worked with many bootstrap entrepreneurs and creatives as well as business owners and professionals who've changed career courses or advanced their own endeavors in comparable ways. Much of what they do mirrors Fullerton's example. They reconcile opposing forces by opening up to serendipity, as she did with video games and nature contemplation. She allowed her identity to shift from a startup founder who was pioneering television entertainment to a university lab leader changing the way video games educate—and changing the way the gaming industry itself can be more inclusive.

You can follow this lead and then cut your own experimental path with an open mindset. But that means you will grapple with ideas and forces that may initially feel contradictory. For instance, you may hold the belief that "good things happen to good people" and then in a short period of time, you might be beset by natural disaster, illness, or another surprising hardship. Or perhaps you have always defined yourself as a struggling writer, but suddenly you start to view yourself as a community organizer. Or perhaps your business project maintains two conflicting markets—one for people who want to meditate, and the other for people who want fitness training—and you're not sure how to reconcile them. In fertile confusion, two conflicting forces, ideas, or concepts might come together to seed this phase of possibility.

Or maybe two parts of your identity seek a new synthesis. Kerra Bolton had built a successful career as a journalist, political pundit, and media communications specialist. As the media communications director for a prominent political figure, she was in North

Carolina's political inner circle and played a part in President Barack Obama's momentous win of that state in 2008. By 2016, she left North Carolina and those roles for Mexico. Her mother died just before she left, and the country's divisive political climate shook Kerra's sense of safety.

As a Black woman, she wanted a new start. She wanted to shed the identity tied to politics and media communications. "Artist" is what kept beckoning her toward a future horizon, but she had little idea how that would happen. During her phase of bewilderment, Bolton stayed open to possibility.

After a quick stint in making masks as an artist, she started publishing bold opinion pieces, including for CNN.com, which brought her notoriety and the attention of Ted Wachtel, founder of the International Institute of Restorative Practices (IIRP). IIRP defines restorative practices as "an emerging social science that studies how to strengthen relationships between individuals as well as social connections within communities." Wachtel hired Bolton as a journalist to travel with filmmaker Cassidy Friedman to document IIRP's effects in the city of Detroit where restorative practices had helped rebuild relationships between the police force and communities of color.

While in Detroit, Bolton was personally moved by the encounters, and Friedman started to turn the lens on Bolton. She became not only the journalist but also an "actor" in the unfolding narrative. That shift in lens awakened Kerra's creativity in an even brighter light that meshed with her strong drive for justice and abiding curiosity in social issues. Fast-forward two years later, and Bolton helped Wachtel produce the award-winning docuseries *Detroit Rising: How the Motor City Becomes a Restorative City*, a project that Bolton says "led to discovering my voice as a filmmaker." Now she is working on *Return of the Black Madonna*, which she notes "follows my experiences learning to swim, dive, and map sunken slave ships with Black marine archaeologists"— with Bolton as the protagonist.

In some ways, Bolton held the space between her roles as journalist, communications specialist, and artist. The once-unknown space between has become an identity of her own making that weaves parts of her new role as documentary filmmaker and actress. Through navigating her bewilderment, she has evolved in her unique way.

That's the wonder of bewilderment.

BEWILDERMENT

For your tracking wonder journey, you can take the opportunity to breathe into your fear reactions, retrain your brain to react to surprise with more creativity and less reactivity, and harness the power of fertile confusion to reshape your creative identity.

The Space Between Breaths

You might recall that one of my early adult insights about wonder came by studying the philosophical book the *Siva Sutras*. This philosophy references a Sanskrit name for that subtle space between two thoughts, two actions, or two breaths. It is called *unmesa*, and in this tradition when you contemplate this space, you might glimpse the nature of consciousness—for a second. In this breathing practice, you keep your attention on the pause between your easeful exhalation and your easeful inhalation.

I invite you to think of this practice this way: When you exhale and your heartbeat slows down, you expel what was no longer flourishing. You let go. When you inhale and your heartbeat speeds up, you take in the possibility of this moment, a breathing in of what could be. Breathe out: *Who were you?* Pause. Breathe in: *Who could you become?* Breathe out: *What was?* Pause. Breathe in: *What could be?*

As you extend the exhalation and center on that slight pause, your heartbeat likely will slow down. Your vagus nerve could be activated, an experience that correlates with feeling more open and compassionate instead of helpless.

I imagine each short pause as an acceptance for this space between the familiar shore of what was and the unknown shore ahead of what could be.

Unmesa also references the moment your eyelids open. In other words, in that pause, thoughts might cease and you might glimpse a new insight. You might glimpse something true and beautiful. For a fleeting moment, wonder might visit.

Live the Question

In times of bewilderment, call upon your young genius. Revisit your young genius traits and memories. Ask yourself a series of questions:

In this time of confusion, what would my young genius do?

What if I could be engaged in activities that brought forward more of my young genius qualities? What would such activities look like? Sound like? Who might I be engaged with?

What is a hard-to-answer question about a topic I am deeply curious about that could propel me through bewildering times?

Write, sketch, doodle, or map responses in your Tracking Wonder notebook. Record passages from readings that seem to speak to your questions. Honor the insights that arise in this space between.

Imagine a Portal of Possibility

Take this invitation if part of your bewilderment stems from questions about your evolving identity. In Lewis Carroll's *Alice's Adventures in Wonderland*, the hookah-toking caterpillar asks the hapless girl, "Who are you?" Her response: "I—I hardly know, sir, just at present—at least I know who I WAS when I got up this morning, but I think I must have been changed several times since then." Ha. Alice perfectly describes how many of us feel, doesn't she? *Who are you?* For the very reason that identity reinvention can be complex, I want to give you a simple yet time-tested exercise.

In your Tracking Wonder notebook, draw two large overlapping circles.

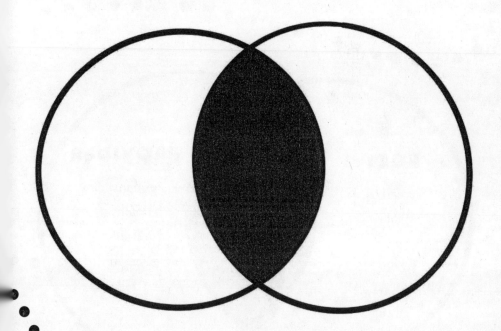

In the left circle, write down the roles you have been playing that might feel constrictive.

In the right circle, write down one or more roles that energize you and that feel expansive. These roles might be ones you've already experienced or ones that you imagine playing.

The space between holds a portal of possibility. Consider Tracy Fullerton or Kerra Bolton. Keep the space in between open for such a portal.

On a separate page, get curious: In what ways might the best of the roles on the left be fertilized and be brought forward in a new form or context? How might these roles not conflict but entwine creatively in a future context?

When you contemplate how a new role or identity might emerge in this open space between, what images surface? Sometimes taking a walk outdoors with this question can seed an idea that you can track.

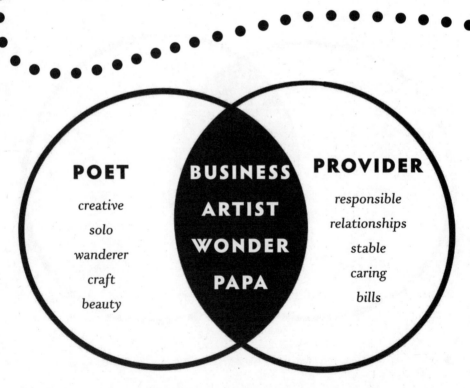

POET

creative

solo

wanderer

craft

beauty

BUSINESS

ARTIST

WONDER

PAPA

PROVIDER

responsible

relationships

stable

caring

bills

Again, I would be foolish and misleading you if I claimed there were "four steps to clarity out of bewilderment." It is true that you can track this facet if you feel the confusion, celebrate the confusion, hold the space between, and fertilize the confusion. Ultimately, though, you make your own map through the woods.

The next chapters reinforce this good news: you don't need to take such a bewildering journey alone.

CHAPTER 7

HOPE,
THE RAINBOW
FACET

THE NATURALIST NIKKI VAN Schyndel once found herself ship-wrecked. Living without any modern technologies on a remote is-land near Vancouver, Canada, for nearly two years, she was on a quest with her adventure partner to capture enough fish to last them through a cold winter. They had journeyed out into the deep ocean to set baited longlines during a sunny day when a sudden squall came up. As their ten-foot-long rowboat bounced along whitecaps in big gusts of wind, water began pouring over the sides of their petite vessel. As she wrote about in her book *Becoming Wild*, Nikki prepared for the worst. She and her partner wrestled them-selves into life jackets that they had previously used as seat cush-ions, since they expected to fly overboard any second. Nikki knew very little about fishing, even less about steering rowboats, but she did know that 20 percent of drowning victims die within two min-utes of water contact because they can't control their shock, which makes them gasp frantically for air. Through the darkening clouds, the two spied an islet close enough to try to row to, so they mus-tered all the strength they had to fight the waves to get to dry land. As they pulled the boat onto the rocky shore, they could feel that they were already in the second stage of hypothermia.

They looked at each other's blue lips, frigid fingers, and pale skin, and began shivering uncontrollably. No warm cabin awaited them. They realized that they would have to weather the night on this tiny sliver of land, so they set about collecting materials for fire and a shelter. Neither had an emergency kit with them—no lighter, no food, no water. Nikki knew this episode was possibly not going to end happily ever after. So what did she do? Instead of panicking, she took a moment to sit quietly. She called on her inner strength to de-termine the best course of action. After listening to her inner genius, she knew they couldn't stay there, but perhaps the energy of fiercely rowing could keep them from advancing their hypothermia.

As they trawled through the waves again, they noticed tiny neon-green sparks, like tiny dancers, exploding off of their oars each time they dragged them through the water. As dark de-scended, they gaped in awe at the magic they were creating with each paddle forward. "It was like a celebration that brightened the long journey home. Watching the dance gave my mind something to love, distracting it from complaints about being soaking wet and dangerously cold," she wrote. Were spirits propelling them to safety? How could something so glorious occur right in the middle of the worst experience of their lives?

This experience of wonder gave the couple strength they didn't know they had. Nikki beamed with gratitude as they began to make out the silhouette of their home in the darkness and knew they would get home safe. She believed something had been watching out for them, turning them from victims into survivors. Later they learned that they had witnessed rare bioluminescent algae that release a blue-green glowing chemical reaction when disturbed, most likely to warn off predators. People have long been fascinated by these sparkles that appear like an aquatic aurora borealis. Their appearance during Nikki's harrowing self-rescue is a reminder of the ways that wonder shows up in the facet of hope.

FACET 4: HOPE

Hope is a reaction spurred by unexpected experiences of wonder that occur amid extreme difficulties and crises. Specifically, hope as a facet of wonder can arise from a surprising moment or sign that lets you see a glimmer (sometimes algae-sized) of possibility toward an otherwise uncertain or dark future. The psychologist and renowned hope researcher C. R. Snyder offers a metaphor. Snyder, who developed the Adult Hope Scale, a model that measures an adult's level of hope, stated, "A rainbow is a prism that sends shards of multicolored light in various directions. It lifts our spirits and makes us think of what is possible. Hope is the same—a personal rainbow of the mind." It's a telling metaphor because the rainbow has been the central study of wonder for centuries among theologians, philosophers, and scientists. Hope is the rainbow facet of wonder.

Both bewilderment and hope as facets of wonder can build fortitude and resilience. Hope, as we will discover, is more than just an optimistic state of mind; it is an action-oriented vision. If we can still track wonder while we face grief, adversity, illness, and other critical setbacks, hope will allow us to find purpose and creativity no matter what the circumstance.

SET YOUR SIGHTS

It turns out that there is a science of hope that has led to many therapeutic practices. Recent research correlates hope with higher academic and athletic performance, higher levels of physical and psychological well-being, improved self-esteem, and enhanced interpersonal relationships. Shane Lopez, a former student of Snyder, said, "Hope is the belief that the future will be better than the present and the belief that you will be able to make it so." In his formulation, to truly access hope, you must have optimism, a sense of personal agency, and plans for how you will act. He found that people who measured high on scales of hopeful attitudes were much more productive. "Hope for the future," he wrote, "pays off today."

People who track hope have commonalities. For one, hopeful people set their sights on future goals, however close or far away. Lopez's research shows that they define and pursue two to three goals doggedly. Even if you think yourself goal averse, consider how this simple act could shift your experience. Setting and taking small steps toward two to three goals provides meaning and purpose under otherwise distressing crises or setbacks.

Hopeful people also tend to interpret adverse events more as challenges than as threats. Hoping, Lopez emphasized, is notably different from wishing. With a wish, the energy behind the thought is more like a magic spell. You don't connect your actions to the desired outcome, which can disempower you. Think of it this way, metaphorically. You're stranded in the middle of an ocean. If you rely only on wishful thinking and optimism, you simply say to yourself, "Everything is going to work out fine. Everything is going to work fine."

Hope, on the other hand, helps you forecast how to get from the middle of the ocean to a safe shore and to take small actions accordingly. Like the people I work with who expect some things to go wrong, hopeful people believe they can overcome those obstacles because they know they can be flexible and find a new route. As the seventeenth-century philosopher Baruch Spinoza understood, both fear and hope are responses to an uncertain future. He wrote, "There is no hope unmingled with fear, and no fear unmingled with hope." Fear and hope can spur each other when you are in danger, as they did van Schyndel in the sea storm.

DAYDREAM DELIBERATELY

Let's track hope a step further with a counterintuitive practice: deliberate daydreaming. Yes, daydreaming. If parents, teachers, or bosses have admonished you for daydreaming, then realize that much of our culture has been as biased against daydreaming as against wonder. Yet in my experience working with and interviewing so many innovative people, I kept wondering why some of them floundered just after launching a dream project, while others flourished. The reasons, I suspected, had little to do with external factors such as financial means, obligations, or sudden setbacks. I thought the difference might have something to do with the individual's degree of intrinsic drive and commitment, especially in the face of such setbacks.

It turns out that they daydream. If you deliberately daydream about your desired future, you could boost your chances of achieving your goals, according to research from Germany. In the study, college students identified a study goal and kept a daydream diary for two weeks. Actively daydreaming helped those students already driven by achievement and excellence. They were the group best able to achieve their study goals.

But *how* you daydream is essential. The psychologist Jerome L. Singer's body of work challenged many of his fellow psychologists' bias against that mind-wandering faculty. In his book *The Inner World of Daydreaming*, Singer distinguishes three different ways to daydream. The first form that Singer identifies is when you might have poor attention control and you use daydreaming as a way to escape some kind of effortful focus. Call it distracted daydreaming. The second kind, called the guilty-dysphoric type, is when your thoughts trend toward anguished fantasies—more like catastrophic nightmares than playful daydreams.

What Singer calls positive-constructive daydreaming is the sweet spot, where we find benefits to daydreaming. Neither fantastical escape nor catastrophic thinking, this playful, artful approach engages your imagination to explore *your* possibilities for a better future, however distant or near. This kind of daydreaming leads to making plans and solving problems in a way that complements Lopez's research on setting your sights on a meaningful goal or two. A component of hope is that you begin to envision actions that will lead to your ultimate aim.

If you don't allow regular time to daydream deliberately, you might feel even more distressed and myopic when it comes to seeing a positive future. Just as night dreaming allows our nervous system to sort of "expel" a lot of unconscious pressure, this type of daydreaming gives our minds space to integrate the daily challenges or hardships we face, especially amid despair.

BE OPEN TO TINY BEAUTIES
TO BUILD RESILIENCE

Following the tragedy of September 11, 2001, some 70 percent of Americans reported feeling depressed, and a large number felt anxiety. Of what use would wonder and other such emotional experiences have under such duress? In 2001, Barbara Fredrickson and other psychologists set up a study to find out. Of the New York City college students they surveyed, they discovered that those who actively sought experiences that piqued their interest or gave them gratitude were less likely to be depressed than their peers who did not seek such experiences. By actively seeking out positive emotions rather than succumbing solely to negative ones, these students had developed the psychological resources—life satisfaction, hope, and tranquility—to successfully navigate crises, both their personal ones and collective ones, such as the tragedy of the September 11 attacks. They had developed resilience.

If you respond with interest amid a crisis, your interest can broaden your awareness to an unusually wide range of new creative possibilities for both personal setbacks and professional solutions. But you must find the things that elicit your interest— things you are excited about and good at doing, for instance, that can build a cascade of more hopeful thoughts.

You might notice how wonder can be a surprise visitor in times of adversity. A yellow monarch landed on the bookshelf of my charred study the morning after our farmhouse burned. That visit was like a timely reset button on my outlook that let me know we would weather the storm. When a hard-to-diagnose neurological disorder forced the writer Elisabeth Tova Bailey to stay prone in bed for months, she feared her life was slipping by. Then a friend brought her a pot of flowers with a hidden stowaway guest, a woodland snail. Almost as still and slow-moving as Bailey, the snail became a source of fascination for the ailing writer, and for the next year, its activities gave her hope and fortitude. She was open to this tiny beauty and followed her interest in it.

That incessant interest stirred Bailey's curiosity, and she gradually mustered enough energy to keep notes and have friends bring her books on Mollusca (snails, slugs, octopi, and other slimy beauties). In her book *The Sound of a Wild Snail Eating*—part memoir, part natural history of snails—Bailey writes that the snail "was adding a welcome focus to my life, and I couldn't think how I would otherwise have passed the hours." Bailey opened the door to wonder and to hope, and then she pursued her interest.

I know when personal despair or a cloudy cynicism weighs you down, it might sound absurd to wait for wonder to visit. But remember a couple of wonder's qualities. Evasive yet pervasive, wonder can be a sort of "now you see it, now you don't" fleeting experience. Wonder can tap on your door, but will you open it? I hope so. Be careful, though: sometimes such a visit can drive you to pursue what others might think is a crazy dream straight to a mountaintop. That was the case with one of my clients of many years.

FOLLOWING HOPE TO THE MOUNTAINTOP

Before she reached forty years old, Lee Rankin had a wild dream to create a farm sanctuary for herself and her two-year-old boy, Will. They would raise alpacas and maybe offer tours to keep business going. Although she grew up with no direct farming experience, the dream seemed within reach when she bought vast farmland atop one of North Carolina's Appalachian Mountains. She hoped that her son would grow up free in the natural world among animals he could care for and people who would care for him.

Only that's not the way the dream turned out, at first. Within the first few years, a contractor hired to renovate the main house died, possibly of a meth overdose, in Lee's basement; the house had to be more or less exorcised; a mountain lion killed the first alpacas to arrive; and brutal winter snowstorms and blizzards threatened the farm and Rankin's dream. And, frankly, the daily grind of slogging through the mud and tending to dying animals was less than bucolic.

So what really drove Rankin to the mountaintop in the first place? She and I pursued this question so that we could figure out how to tell her story in a captivating way. She grew up in the social circles of Lexington, Kentucky, where appearances matter. When Rankin, unmarried, got pregnant at age thirty-seven, having just come off of successful treatment for breast cancer, she had little support. Despite her new boyfriend's wishes for her not to have the baby, despite her aloof father's request to "make the situation disappear," and despite one doctor's advice not to risk triggering the cancer's return, she had the baby. She knew she couldn't raise her son, Will, in a place where he wasn't accepted, but where would she go? And how would she make a living? Something burned inside her, she said, "a desire I could not articulate, let alone fulfill, at the time."

One day at the Kentucky State Fair, wonder visited. She locked eyes with an alpaca, to be exact. The creature, fuzzy like a teddy bear, seemed to radiate warmth and humility. The alpaca, quiet creature of the plains, was giving her the empathetic gaze she had always wanted to feel from her family. The depth and power of its eyes dropped right into Lee's heart, she said, and took her breath away. When their gaze broke, Lee held up her hand as the alpaca slowly leaned in to softly nuzzle her. This was her wondrous moment of discovery and of hope. It awakened a hard-to-articulate yearning.

Shortly after this encounter, surprising even herself, Lee announced to her family and friends that she wanted to raise alpacas on a farm. This came out of the blue to everyone. Despite their doubts and fears, Lee chased after her vision and made it happen. Over twenty years later, Apple Hill Farm is home to alpacas, horses, cows, chickens, dogs, donkeys, and goats—many of them rescue animals. Their growing team produces a high-quality yarn that's prized for its softness and durability. They also offer tours, and now advise other groups looking to get into agritourism.

But what happens when we feel as if wonder misplaced our address and won't come knocking anytime soon? One beautiful thing about being human is that we can track wonder when it doesn't seem to track us.

SURROUND YOURSELF WITH HOPE

Wonder can meet you on the other side of grief and hand you back the hope to live more fully.

By 2015, the artist Nick Cave had become more than a legendary and versatile alternative-rock songwriter and vocalist. "Controlled hysteria" is how a blues musician once described Cave's honest, hypnotic baritone and his narrative prose songs. Since 1983, when he joined the band the Bad Seeds, the Australian-born Cave has produced some fifteen albums, landed a song on a Harry Potter film soundtrack, starred in two films, penned a novel and a collection of plays, and won the Venice Film Festival's Gucci Award for writing the script to the Australian western film *The Proposition*.

> **Wonder can meet you on the other side of grief and hand you back the hope to live more fully.**

Apparently no one advised Cave to stay in his lane and stick to one thing, or if they did, this intense, lanky style icon apparently ignored them. One UK journalist interviewing Cave in 2001 wrote, "His muse, the creative impulse, whatever you like to call it, is what separates him from his contemporaries, what elevates him to the heights of the truly great songwriters, what keeps him sane. . . ." By the time of that 2001 interview, not incidentally, Cave had married Susie Bick, an actress and fashion company founder. When they had twin sons, Earl and Arthur, Cave's muse became even more disciplined. He showed up for work at a desk, describing himself as a "nine-to-five man."

But in 2015, Cave lost his way when tragedy befell his family. Cave's son Arthur fell sixty feet from a chalk cliff above Ovingdean Gap, about three miles from where the family lives in Brighton, England. He died, at age fifteen, of head trauma and related injuries.

Cave, a hands-on father, was devastated. In the 2016 documentary *One More Time with Feeling*, which revolves around the artist and the catastrophic aftermath of his son's death, Cave said: "I just don't have any handle on things anymore. It's frightening." He also lost his grip on lyrical writing and on his creative process in general. Wayward, he no longer had the daily discipline to show up at his desk and work. For someone accustomed to years of such habits, this period of grief must have been profoundly disorienting.

You've likely had your share of setbacks and losses that sent you far away from the path you had imagined. Emotional storms can squash your desire to pursue any kind of meaningful work or activity. When your world loses its vibrant colors, when your life has lost its uplifting soundtrack, what will bring you back so you can make the work you're here for?

For Cave, the first element was sincere, honest connection. Cave's fans reached out with epic support to the artist they loved. When we suffer emotional flatness or despair, social isolation especially can deepen the suffering, but Cave recognized a way out. He and Susie realized they weren't alone in their suffering. Then Cave responded in kind to his fans by starting *The Red Hand Files*, a blog in which he takes a fan's question and responds in an eloquent letter. Named after his signature 1994 song "Red Right Hand," which itself was inspired by John Milton's epic poem *Paradise Lost*, the term refers to the vengeful hand of God. Cave realized that everyone shared suffering. Stripped of any slick promotion or connection to selling albums or events, Cave holds true to the blog's premise: "You can ask me anything. There will be no moderator. This will be between you and me. Let's see what happens."

Hopeful people reach out for support and help. One key component, the hope researcher Lopez found, was that hopeful people spread hope, so it is important to surround yourself with hopeful people. Consider your own dark situations. When you cannot see a positive way forward, you might be tempted to close the doors and drapes on the world, so to speak. You might want to suffer alone. Yet as the stories in this chapter illustrate, moments of wonder expand your world.

Remember the image of Indra's Net? It is a vast net that stretches across the universe with a glimmering jewel at each node. When in dire doubt about my place in the world or the future, I step back in my imagination and see myself not as an island but as one of those jewels connected with all of the universe's other jewels. When your future seems disheartening and you feel alone, you also might step back and remember the jewels in your life: the friend with the right outlook who's a phone call away, the stranger at the café who picks up your tab for no ulterior motive, the colleague who quietly listens.

CREATE YOUR WAY TO HOPE

But what especially brought Nick Cave back to his life's work is revealed in the first post of *The Red Hand Files*. A fan named Jakub asked Cave how his process of writing was going following his son's death. With characteristic honesty and eloquence, Cave described his and Susie's situation: "[F]or a year it had been difficult to work out how to write, because the centre had collapsed and Susie and I had been flung to the outer reaches of our lives. We were kind of outlanders floating in deep space . . . lost in narcissism and self-absorption."

What was the center of their lives? Cave said this: "In an artist's case (and perhaps it is the same for everybody) I would say it is a sense of wonder. Creative people in general have a great propensity for wonder. Great trauma can rob us of this, the ability to be awed by things. . . . We all needed to draw ourselves back to a state of wonder." Cave says he found his way back to the center of wonder by working and connecting with his community of friends and fans. They gave him hope. Hope did not dispel his pain, but it gave him the energy to keep creating.

Keeping yourself lit up and alive, renewed and ready is not easy. Cave had to work at reclaiming wonder, in a sense. He wrote at home instead of at his office, and he allowed for a stream of thoughts, images, and ideas to accumulate. "I found with some practice," he said, "the imagination could propel itself beyond the personal into a state of wonder. In doing so the color came back to things with a renewed intensity and the world seemed clear and bright and new." Note here that he said that it came with some practice.

Cave would eventually pull together enough songs from snippets and spontaneous threads to produce the album *Ghosteen*, an album of wonder amid grief. *Ghosteen* references in part his son's presence after death. His experience with grief echoes in a sense what the psychologist Martha Nussbaum writes: "In grief there is, I think, often a kind of wonder—in which one sees the beauty of the lost person as a kind of radiance standing at a very great distance from us." In one song, "Night Raid," from the album, Cave sings with backup that "we all rose from wonder" and would never surrender to defeat. The album does not aim to send listeners into sadness, per se, but, as Cave wrote a fan, to reach toward "the jubilant and hopeful beyond." This album's gorgeous expression of a father's grief for his dead son so disarms me and unravels my heart that when I listen to it, I find it hard to be near either of my daughters. I imagine Cave's renewed focus on his community and on the songs that ultimately made up *Ghosteen* as Cave's way of deliberate daydreaming. He created his way through the stormy sea, one melody at a time. The pacing, I imagine, must have been slow and steady, not unlike the snail that lured Bailey's interest and brought her faculties back to life.

Maybe you have or can find a meaningful creative endeavor on which to keep a steady focus amid adversity. Such a creative endeavor can be a kind of multicolored life raft. You can be experimental. If you're a teacher feeling burnout or some other melee, you could direct part of your attention to refreshing a learning unit that could renew your and your students' interest. If you're a manager whose company has experienced setbacks and duress, focus on one small way you could bring a little joy to company meetings.

SPREAD HOPE

With Lee Rankin's dream, there's another meta-story to note: For her first few years of operation, Lee hid her origin story from her new community. The farm website was a wall of text that conveyed a generic history, provided basic tour information, and showed no photographs of people. She was professionally camouflaging her identity and story to blend in because she feared people might judge her as a single mother. The thought of drawing attention to herself repelled her. Yet she felt creatively unfulfilled and professionally frustrated because the annual tour numbers and shop sales weren't hitting the mark. Slowly, though, things changed. First, Rankin got the courage to shape her story of hope into a memoir, which in turn gave her courage to share part of her story with local chamber of commerce and agritourism organizations who invited her to speak. People told her how touched they were. Through this act of vulnerability, she felt connected to her colleagues, neighbors, and fellow farmers in ways she hadn't for years. Maybe her example of staying true to her convictions and pursuing the craziest of dreams helped them understand their wild stories, too.

Emboldened, Rankin took hope to another level. She worked with our team to rebrand the farm website, showcasing her story in the right place and framing the farm's mission, which is about real connection. Within months of the new site's launch, people were drawn to the farm like moths to light in times of darkness. Radio and television show hosts saw a newsworthy story that was more than a local attraction. ESPN later featured the alpacas during a college football tournament called the Sun Belt Bowl. The farm, named one of North Carolina's top tourist attractions, received awards from the local tourism organization. A couple of years later, she had become a statewide go-to expert on agritourism, which led to developing her signature Agritourism Works workshops. The business numbers tell a complementary story: tour numbers and revenue have tripled, they've broken records for their sales of yarn every year, and Rankin spends more time writing, teaching, and leading than she ever had in years past.

And Rankin's hard-to-articulate desire? She was able to express that yearning that she had and that so many of the people working and visiting the farm also shared: a desire to belong. What she longed for was to belong to a real family, a farm family made by her, her son Will, and a growing community of people and animals, together.

Algae opened naturalist Nikki van Schyndel to hope, a snail piqued Elisabeth Tova Bailey's interest enough to hope, an alpaca surprised Lee Rankin to hope, and community plus the creative act itself allowed Nick Cave the hope to come home to himself. The naturalist, the writer, the farmer, and the musician all acknowledged the tiny beauties, stayed open to hope, and ultimately shared what came out of their adversity. They each in essence are a jewel in the net, a rainbow who in turn spreads hope.

I think of Czeslaw Milosz. Born and raised in war-torn Poland in the early twentieth century, his childhood was rife with memories of his father away at battle, of him and his mother fleeing warring factions, and even at one moment escaping being shot at. As a student of poetry and politics in his twenties, Milosz lived in Warsaw when Hitler invaded Poland and bombed Warsaw. Milosz escaped. Eventually, for his body of work, Milosz earned the Nobel Prize in Literature. In one poem from one of his final volumes, he wrote that even among a life of bitterness, confusion, and evil, "Wonder kept seizing me, and I recall only wonder."

I think of the poets in all of us, that natural part of us that can muster from the muck something beautiful and exquisite and proffer it to a crying child, a dying parent, or a despairing group of people. All of us—you, me—can keep being seized by wonder, and all of us can spread hope.

HOPE

Track this facet of wonder, the personal rainbow of the mind, especially when you're facing adversity, crises, or constant blocks in advancing your dreams. Let's start painting your mind with new hues.

Pursue Your Interest—or Let It Pursue You

The greatest enemy of hope is apathy, that numb state of not caring about anything. To track hope, then, it's important to keep part of your attention on something you're interested in. Remember Barbara Fredrickson's research with the post-9/11 college students? If you actively direct your attention toward what you are uniquely interested in, your emotional, cognitive, and social resources can build and broaden. You'll be able to harness your emotions, capture hopeful insights, and connect with people who genuinely care about you.

If you already have a project or endeavor that holds your attention, then find a way that's right for you to give it space. A snail, an alpaca, or algae might not visit you, but if you stay open and curious to such surprising "visitors," you just might get an intuitive signal to pay attention to something unique. Once you acknowledge the interest, treat it like a companion on your journey. How can you connect your interest to something that will get you actively moving forward toward a hopeful goal?

Set Your Sights on a Simple, Meaningful Pursuit Goal

Make a simple, meaningful goal you can move forward on and attain within the next three weeks. Setting a goal requires imagining the future. When you're under duress, or if you're not accustomed to pursuing specific goals consistently, I recommend you limit the scope of your goals to three weeks or less at a time. For most of us, a lot happens within three weeks. Here are some examples:

Read one book on my topic of interest within three weeks.

Write my future bio that reflects what happened because I pursued my interest.

By the end of three weeks, I will have two hours every morning to myself with clear boundaries set with my family.

By the end of three weeks, I will have reserved one hour in the evening to read offline in my area of interest before bed.

We pursue what we care about, and sometimes we must remind ourselves why we care. So I recommend you elaborate on your goal as much as possible so you feel a personal connection to it. What does pursuing this goal mean to you? What good feelings and outcomes drive you? Imagine you've reached the other side of the rainbow—even if it's only three weeks away. How does that feel? You might return to the previous chapter on curiosity. The invitation "Connect Your Curiosity to What You Care About" offers further intuitive questions if you need more guidance.

Share It

Remember how important it was for Nick Cave to share his journey with his community and what happened to Lee Rankin's dream once she actively shared her story? Hope ripples. Each week, the members in my Tracking Wonder Inner Circle MasterMind group commit to our Accountability Agreement. There is always something unpredictable occurring for one or more of this group of brilliant, wholehearted human beings that could waylay their schemes, but no matter what, they agree to provide one another with weekly responses to these questions:

What can you celebrate from this past week with regard to your life and work? In a sentence or two, what is a relevant challenge you're facing or tension you're experiencing? How are you taking agency and bringing your young genius to work?

What is your priority three-week pursuit goal or larger biannual goal you're focusing on for this coming week? What actions will you take to move closer toward it?

How will you let wonder intervene this week?

Even though we post these updates in a private online forum, these Accountability Agreement updates buoy us tremendously. We cheer one another on and, when needed, offer one another resources, guidance, and support.

Leo Babauta, a former client known especially for his vastly popular *Zen Habits* blog, told me he has always considered his community of readers as "collaborators" of sorts. After we worked together to facilitate a big brand transition that would require a couple of years of behind-the-scenes work, he posted an email to a group of us he calls his "Sacred Council." Each weekly update included three bullet points: his intentions from the past week, how he did with those intentions, and what his intentions are for the next week. We recipients were never required or expected to respond. The importance of the action was more in Leo knowing that he was holding himself accountable to someone outside of himself.

Your Hope Horizon Sheet

Use this worksheet to help you actively track hope in your life, creative work, and relationships. Notice that the scope of this goal reaches as far as three months, instead of three weeks. You keep the scope of your goal close enough that it's attainable and far enough that it brings out the best in your young genius.

YOUR HOPE HORIZON: What is one meaningful goal you aim to reach within the next three months or less? Examples from our clients:

- By March, publish and deliver a course for people returning to the workforce.

- By August, our team will have defined quarterly goals with plans of action in marketing and customer delight.

- In six weeks, submit an article on the power of restorative exercises in the workplace.

MY HOPE HORIZON GOAL:

_____

_____

_____

_____

DELIBERATELY DAYDREAM THE PATHWAY: Take a fifteen-minute walk and imagine yourself taking small actions and steps toward your goal every day. The motion of walking and sensory stimulation will activate your imagination. When you return from the walk, write in as much detail as possible about what you see yourself actively doing.

What small actions can you take that will start moving you closer toward this goal?

MY DELIBERATE DAYDREAM INSIGHTS:

_____

_____

_____

_____

ACKNOWLEDGE THE CHALLENGE OR INTERNAL
OBSTACLE: Remember your downer mind patterns?
Yeah, those. Write down in detail what one key internal
obstacle or downer pattern might get in your way.
Admitting it and externalizing it on the page can dispel
its unconscious hold on you. One Inner Circle MasterMind
member had a huge, tearful breakthrough when she
acknowledged her false narrative that her earning a
comfortable living would mean she was greedy and
heartless. That purge allowed us to take the next step.

MY INTERNAL OBSTACLE:

_____

_____

_____

_____

_____

_____

_____

_____

ACTIVATE MY YOUNG GENIUS: Affirm to yourself your three young genius traits and how one or more of those traits can serve you on this journey. How will you draw upon your core capabilities to finesse that obstacle and step wisely and steadily closer toward your goal?

MY GENIUS MANEUVER:

When I face . . .

_____

_____

_____

_____

I will . . .

_____

_____

_____

_____

_____

CHAPTER 8

CONNECTION, THE FLOCK FACET

OUR YEARNING TO SYNC

SOMETHING IN ME YEARNS to bond with each of my daughters on their terms, yet I bomb over and over again. Why can we human beings fail so epically at connecting, let alone collaborating, with one another? If it's true that wonder is not kid's stuff but radical grown-up stuff—a belief that gets daily reinforced—then could experiences of wonder and curiosity help us work, create, and support *one another* better?

One spring afternoon, my younger daughter Alethea and I took a walk in a nearby park. She had been reporting to me what she knew about butterflies, how one side of their wings displays beautiful colors and designs, and how the other side helps them blend in.

"Oh, right," I said, "That's camouflage."

"I know," she said and went on.

I'm still learning to listen, to ask questions, and to shut up—to not "teach" my child at every freaking moment. It's a humbling habit to break that gets in the way of so many grown-up relationships. Sometimes a person just wants to share what she's learning to be true in the world without some know-it-all topping her emergent knowledge.

As if on cue, Alethea suddenly stopped and said, "Listen, Papa." I did so. From one set of trees erupted a hidden yet gossipy chorus of birds, boisterous and musical. She drew me closer a few steps, and then the treetops exploded as black swirls emerged, lifted and dipped, twisted and swirled like an animated van Gogh painting. For several minutes, Alethea and I stood spellbound with delight as we watched a speedy amoeba-like cloud made up of black dots shape-shift through the air. Hundreds of starlings syncopated a midair dance. Where words so often get in the way, a shared visceral experience of wonder bonded us. For the rest of the evening, Alethea and I could recount the experience. My daughter and I had, as it were, "a moment."

Scientists are still uncertain about what drives this aviary phenomenon known as murmuration, but our fascination with it reflects, I believe, this human yearning to sync up. We rarely experience that kind of selfless, unplanned collective improvisation, and yet many of us long to feel connected to something greater than ourselves that bonds us with other people. That longing leads us to participate in organized sports, performing arts, dance, musical bands and ensembles, and ventures. If you have that longing, heed it. We need it.

As the stories, studies, and examples in this chapter reveal, when you track this facet of wonder through various forms of collaboration, you can grow as a human being who can navigate experimental uncertainty with more grace. In short, you do it better together.

But fair warning. Those idealized moments of what we might call co-flow—like jazz musicians improvising in superb harmony—are rare. To experience co-flow usually requires more preparation and practice than what those starling spectacles imply. And this, it turns out, is precisely where tracking connection can come into play.

FACET 5: CONNECTION

Wonder isn't exclusive to solo moments when you're witnessing fireflies orchestrate a light symphony in a meadow or gleaning a serendipitous insight to your most pressing problem. Wonder is also relational and brings adaptive advantage. Recall in chapter 1 that we considered how experiences of wonder help us adapt, survive, and thrive. It bears reminding here that the influential philosopher Martha Nussbaum of the University of Chicago has made a case for wonder's role in our ethical lives. She suggests that wonder gives rise to other emotions, such as compassion and love, that draw us toward others. Wonder suspends our judgments and opens us up to receive the beautiful difference of another human being—whether a stranger or someone we've known for years.

Connection is the powerful flock facet of wonder that fuels our co-creation with others. On every level, from the physiological to the intellectual to the spiritual, connection can dissolve our biases against others. It allows us to glimpse what is true, real, and beautiful about someone else. That opening cracks us open to what is possible among us. When we understand how to harness this power in supportive packs, it will amplify our endeavors and support our creative lives.

CLOSE THE BELONGING GAP

Prolonged isolation could speed up our death, according to mounting studies. In an article in the *Harvard Business Review*, Vivek H. Murthy, the former surgeon general of the United States, wrote, "Loneliness and weak social connections are associated with a reduction in lifespan similar to that caused by smoking fifteen cigarettes a day and even greater than that associated with obesity." If it's true that, as the *New York Times* commentator David Brooks suggests, "social isolation may be the central challenge of our era"; if it's true that 40 percent of Americans report feeling lonely on a regular basis (up from 20 percent twenty years ago); and if it's true that college students after the year 2000 are up to 40 percent less empathetic than college students were before, then how can we diverse human beings come together to create and collaborate better?

I'm sure you've experienced this gap at times yourself, as the formal ways in which we typically gather and socialize have decreased over the past few decades, especially for older people. We connect more on online platforms and less at cafés or dinner tables. When we talk about connection, we often talk less about intimate moments and more about Wi-Fi speed. There is a hunger among some of us, though, to counter these trends.

Could a new conception of love help? In her book *Love 2.0*, the psychologist Barbara Fredrickson explains that our bodies, shaped by long-term evolution, do not respond in the same ways to the symbols of love across physical distance as they do to eye contact, touch, gestures, and full embracing. We're not getting the mirrored postures and real-time sensory contact that we relied on for millennia to stay bonded to our small survival groups. If we are in the same physical space with other people and enjoying mostly positive interactions, though, we typically feel safe and secure. So with more positive physical connections, people become happier, healthier, and more fulfilled.

So what is love 2.0? In Fredrickson's reconception of connection, she suggests that love is not just felt by one individual. Instead, it is a resonance between people. "Love unfolds and reverberates between and among people—*within* interpersonal transactions," she writes, "and thereby belongs to all parties involved, and to the metaphorical connective tissue that binds them together, albeit temporarily. . . . More than any other positive emotion, then, love belongs not to one person but pairs or groups of people. It resides within connections." Love is *connection*, Fredrickson says. And love can occur in a wondrous instant that you share with anyone. "It's even the fondness and sense of shared purpose you might unexpectedly feel with a group of strangers who've come together to marvel at a hatching of sea turtles or cheer at a football game," she writes.

Wonder, in turn, gives rise to our capacity for unmediated compassion, empathy, and love. That is, it's our very capacity to be in wonder toward another human being—without desire for gain from that person—that allows us to connect without shields and armor. If we can orient our days around authentically connecting with others—in our work, within our families, while we are out on a trail in the woods—we boost our capacity to deepen our relationships and our collective potential.

> **It's our very capacity to be in wonder toward another human being—without desire for gain from that person—that allows us to connect without shields and armor.**

SEEK ENSEMBLE CONSCIOUSNESS

My client Amelia Terrapin had such an epiphany about the role of connection in her work as a dancer and science educator. Terrapin began her career working in dance companies, where she experienced ways of achieving high levels of group connection among the dancers' ensemble. She brings that wisdom to her company, Mobius Method, which promotes movement-based connection for schools and organizations. They draw upon principles of nature because nature, they say, "connects us to feelings of wonder, curiosity, and care for the Earth."

Like the choreographed starling show my daughter and I witnessed, an ensemble of dancers works in a co-creative, improvised process in which all participants complement one another with their mutual contributions. The skill of learning to flow in such an ensemble is what Terrapin teaches. "Ensembles create spaces of possibility," she said. "When people move and play together, they gain a new perspective, a new lens to examine how they work as a team in other situations."

When Terrapin developed a movement-based science curriculum for school kids, she was surprised by what she was drawn to—tracking the self-awareness and relationships formed as part of the exercises. She described how she was teaching a unit about the solar system and invited students to make up sixteen counts of a dance that performed the relationship among the sun, the earth, and the moon. "Through this simple choreography process," she said, "the students are forming the kind of rich, co-creative trusting relationship that we do in the dance studio as well, because of the nature of how they are working together."

The results in learning were impressive. Teachers told Terrapin afterward about students who might usually not focus as well or had difficulty mastering concepts as quickly as other students. In movement, their different strengths could be celebrated. For children not typically successful in a traditional classroom environment, they could shine before their peers and see themselves differently, too.

When the group can "verbalize" what happened in the exercise with their bodies and their minds, they feel more openness and curiosity. Terrapin's work taps into what psychologists call physiological synchrony. People interacting tend to synchronize their gestures, their heart rates, even their hormones, which researchers believe makes people trust one another and feel closer.

In such ensemble experiences, wonder arises by communicating through movement as much as in words. And when we experience wonder together and then discuss it, the whole experience in turn becomes inherently connective. As Amelia puts it, "I feel the most connected to you if I get to hear you talk about the thing that elicits wonder for you than if you're telling me about something you're not experiencing wonder with." For the teams and students that Amelia coaches, the syncopation heightens their inherent abilities and brings forward their most fully embodied work.

BUST BIAS WITH WONDER

Sometimes this ensemble connection is a bit tricky to bring forth. We get inhibited in our ability to merge and murmur with one another. Some complex human wiring gets in the way. Consider the adaptive unconscious, a view of the unconscious mind posed by the cognitive psychologist Daniel Wagner and furthered by the psychologist Timothy Wilson. This deeply layered portion of the human mind inherited from millennia helps us survive, adapt, and grow each day. It works quickly, instinctively, and reactively. As thousands of sensory data points swirl through your conscious awareness in any minute—a hum, shapes and patterns, a brush against the skin—your adaptive unconscious automatically categorizes the hum as the noise from a fan, shapes and patterns as chairs and a fan, and the brush against the skin as a fan breeze. You don't have to think consciously about identifying these things all day long, thankfully. Here's the tricky thing about our wiring: Our adaptive unconscious also loves to pin down ideas and people. It often leads to reinforcing stereotypes. Its job is to size up.

Think of this unconscious bias as the Bias Box, unique to each of us. Our Bias Box is our mind's automatic categorizer that boxes in things *and people*. Recall the last time you were in a meeting. Team meetings often are unhealthy in part because people unwittingly peg other people: "Oh, there goes Ralph with all of his ideas about changing the world. (Eye roll.) How many minutes before Melanie talks about safety, finances, and not taking risks? (Sigh.)" Sound familiar? Yet, what are Ralph and Melanie thinking? Is it possible that we have overlooked the nuance and complexity in their formulations? Or is there some curious question we can ask them that would bring their thinking to a different level? Why are we so quick to write off people?

I don't mean to bias shame here. I've studied and learned so much about biases because I've become aware of how rapidly *my* mind forms them, as all our minds do. But I invite you to take stock of your own relation to differences. It's funny how we humans can create divisions between us based upon even simple matters of taste (What movies do you like? What clothes do you wear? What spiritual podcasts do you listen to?). The brain's amygdala can light up when threatened by difference and discomfort. A part of our brain's defensiveness seeks sameness. It's that part of us that pursues ideas that comfort and reinforce our sense of what is true and real. And it's the same part of us that tries to make friends, lovers, children, and collaborators act like us, think like us, make like us, look like us, communicate like us, and pray like us. By dominating others into sameness, though, we ironically can foster divisiveness.

To advance your best work and most helpful ideas in this fractured world requires that you sometimes deliberately steer your adaptive unconscious, with its urges to box in other people and their contributions.

BE OPEN AND CURIOUS

Even the most open-minded creative people among us unknowingly box in other people and their ideas, often to the detriment of collaborations. Ask Ahmir "Questlove" (sometimes written as ?uestlove) Thompson. Best known as the hip-hop Grammy-winning band the Roots' co-frontman and drummer, Questlove is also a master collaborator. Since 2009, the Roots have served as the in-house band first for the television show *Late Night with Jimmy Fallon* and currently for *The Tonight Show Starring Jimmy Fallon*. That gig means they often must be ready to accompany a wide range of musicians. During the first year on *Late Night*, the Roots backed up a lot of new bands coming out of Brooklyn. Questlove had critiqued most of these bands, saying that they had a singular sound and, worse in his mind, a singular attitude: "Brooklyn hipster."

For one show, as Questlove recounts in his memoir, *Late Night* had booked the band Dirty Projectors from Brooklyn, and the Roots were scheduled to back them up. To give you an idea of what might have been happening in Questlove's mind, consider *LA Weekly* culture critic Ben Westhoff's scathing assessment here: "[M]ost of today's 20 and 30-something bands from Silver Lake [LA] and Williamsburg [Brooklyn] sound shockingly similar. They're all playing variations of retro garage and soul music—or bringing glockenspiels and choirs on incestuous nationwide tours—all the while clad in vintage garb likely infested with lice." Ouch.

Questlove's mind had prejudiced him. Yet on this particular night in 2009, Dirty Projectors chose a song "When the World Comes to an End." The number opens with female vocalists altering and overlaying their vocalizations as if three different species of exotic birds had learned to entwine the tapestry of their tones. If human voices could imitate birds' in-sync murmuration, this would be it. Questlove admitted that he suspected some behind-the-scenes synthesizer was manipulating the Dirty Projectors' complex rhythms.

That is, until after the performance. Outside of Questlove's dressing room, the women performed spontaneously and acoustically for him and other Roots members. They listened, just really listened. Something happened. He doesn't use this word, but I think wonder cracked open Questlove's bias. For a fleeting moment, he heard and saw the truth, the reality, and the lingering beauty of Dirty Projectors. His genius could see their genius. As an inveterate wonder tracker, Questlove then seized upon that insight. He invited Dirty Projectors to play at an upcoming Roots show and then brought them into their next album, *How I Got Over*.

It's worth asking how many opportunities you might miss with other people because of your Bias Box. The good news is you can trip your wiring and unbox a potential collaborator. You can foster wonder and curiosity instead, which is exactly Questlove's advice, too, when collaborating: "Be open and curious." Questlove's advice reinforces Terrapin's ensemble work: bring forward the two foundational facets of wonder: openness and curiosity.

OPEN UP; DON'T SIZE UP

Suppose we were able to share meanings freely without a compulsive urge to impose our view or conform to those of others and without distortion and self-deception. Would this not constitute a real revolution in culture?

DAVID BOHM

physicist and author of *Changing Consciousness*

Conversation can be a form of co-flowing, an approximate experience of being in human murmuration. You've likely had that experience with a friend, spouse, or colleague when you felt that you two just "clicked" in conversation. When in a free-flowing conversation of ideas, our sense of time stretches because everyone stays focused as their wits come into play to further the conversation stream.

In fact, neuroscientists have measured people's brains in conversation. The better the communication, the better the sync in a speaker's brain waves and a listener's brain waves. Miriam Steele, a professor of psychology at the New School in New York, studies those moments between parent and child when there's full attunement. She calls these "snatches of magic," as reported in the journalist Kate Murphy's book *You're Not Listening: What You're Missing and Why It Matters.*

In an interview on the *Good Life Project Podcast*, Murphy further explained that these moments are "like this marvelous dance where you're at the same rhythm, and you know what your partner's doing."She compares such conversations to being in a line dance, "and you become greater than yourself. You are part of this great organism moving. It's pure joy." She suggests that we're wired for such transpersonal experiences because they help us survive on this planet through cooperation. But the key is that each partner is mutually interested. There has to be a reciprocal curiosity and flow that builds something greater than the two individuals. To reach that magic, you must interrupt the biases that limit your beliefs about your conversation partner and yourself.

Not all conversations are equal. In the book *Conversational Intelligence*, the organizational anthropologist Judith Glaser distinguishes between conversations that trigger our stress reactions and those that activate our capacity for trust and empathy. There's a body chemistry of conversations, she notes, and unhealthy ones cause distrust and avoidance. Yet we can have wholly expansive encounters with each other. When we have supportive interactions, we feel safe and open, partially because of the release of the bonding hormone oxytocin and the pleasurable neurotransmitters dopamine and serotonin. We think at a higher level, literally using the more highly evolved parts of our brains, which Glaser says is the key to communicating in ways that transform and shape our shared reality with another. Because oxytocin levels spike and descend more quickly than does the hormone released in defense (cortisol), it has less impact on us. We require vastly more positive interactions with someone if we are going to harmonize. If you can keep the chemistry of conversation in mind, you can direct your speech—and perhaps more importantly, your listening—toward trust.

More than any research, though, I have learned most about this facet of wonder through my direct experiences with other people. Several years ago, I attended a four-day "summer camp for grown-ups" that a friend and Good Life Project founder Jonathan Fields hosted. When Jonathan and I met for coffee before the camp, we spent two hours talking as much about our daughters as ideas. I knew I liked this guy. What was there to fear in a simple camp experience? I loved summer camp as a boy, and I trusted Jonathan.

But when I showed up late, I found four hundred people from around the world clustered in a courtyard and on a field outside the dining hall, chatting and hanging out and having a great time. I knew no one except Jonathan—who's more of an introvert than I am, so he was probably hiding out somewhere while his talented team of extroverts handled the logistics. I took a deep breath and walked down a narrow aisle of the crowd, hoping to catch a friendly eye or familiar face or kind soul who would wave me into their conversation. No such luck. Twice I went down that aisle, and then you know what I did? I made a beeline across the meadow, behind the cabins, and into the woods.

"What was I thinking?" I said to myself. "Four days with four hundred strangers and sleeping in a camp dorm room!" My Bias Box ramped up—only in my direction. After years of speaking, facilitating, and teaching to many audiences, suddenly among this cast of strangers something tender in me felt exposed. That best hit on my internal radio station WRRY, "You're No Good," started playing. Part of my primal brain also was likely sizing up these strangers in terms of "friend or foe." Then I took a deep breath, gazed up at the towering pines, and said to myself, "Open up; don't size up." What if I just opened up to everyone, no agenda, and had open conversations in which I just listened to who they are and the stories that brought them here? I decided that was my main intent for being there—to connect and listen to people's stories. It ended up being one of the richest social experiences I've ever had, as I listened to a story of a woman doctor from Kenya, a health activist from London, and more. Many friendships bloomed.

Two years later, I led a workshop on tracking wonder at the same event. Over ninety entrepreneurs signed up for the first one. As I told them that story of walking through what felt like a social gauntlet during my first time at the camp, many heads nodded in recognition. They seemed relieved that I called out what they felt, too. But then something else happened that surprised me. Of the different exercises and mini trainings I led them through, one especially moved them. I call it a Wonder Talk. They paired off, sat a foot apart squarely facing each other, made eye contact, breathed together, and then in a dyad fashion, they alternated roles as speaker and listener. The speaker recalled a place in their heart that had brought them joy—whether a place from childhood or a place visited last week or in their own backyard. They were to use as much descriptive imagery as possible—the texture of air, the certain shade of light—and emphasize how they felt. No analysis.

The quality of the listener made all the difference. The listener repeated to themselves, "Open up; don't size up," and I guided them to "Listen with your feet." That is, I asked listeners not to grasp for what they're hearing nor anticipate in their minds what they need to say back to the speaker in order to add value. Instead, if they dropped part of their attention to their feet, then chances are they would listen in a more whole-bodied way. Speakers only had three minutes each, and yet many pairs appeared near-instantly intimately connected.

I've repeated variations of Wonder Talks at many conferences, events, organizations, and keynotes. Tears surface. Friendships form. A startup founder in Austin reported back that he uses the principles of "Open up; don't size up" and "Listen with your feet" with his managers. In those three minutes, people experience each other in a new, truer, and beautiful way. In the space between us, wonder appears.

DIT BEATS DIY: ON PACKS

One cultural message can get in our way of connecting, let alone flocking: do it yourself. In our digital era, there's a big emphasis on the DIY philosophy that encourages individuals to design, build, and modify things without help from experts, assistants, or peers. Yes, our ever-increasing digital technology democratizes access. You can save money, learn new skills, and feel satisfaction from completing projects that might have otherwise been daunting or exorbitant. Yet complete DIY is a harmful myth. Ambitious people begin to believe that if they genuinely are a brave soul, they must stick it out on their own and figure everything out solo. That myth can turn out to be ironically expensive, frustrating, and self-limiting.

If you've succumbed to the counterproductive DIY myth, open up to another possibility. Imagine how expansive it could be to share your dream with one or more people who get it, support it, and move it forward. Take a few moments to let yourself observe what that might feel like.

I believe that DIY may just be the first formation of an even more powerful philosophy of do it together (DIT). Imagine two DIY masters working on a project together—or a whole team of people each driven by independence and yet they each know they can make unique contributions, amplifying the impact of their shared projects. What if almost anyone you meet could become a potential collaborator, love 2.0–style?

DIT also challenges what we assume to be true about creative originality and solo creative minds, as if all scientific and artistic breakthroughs occur within the confines of single minds locked away in deep solitude. You don't create anything valuable to others alone. There is another way.

This idea of DIT sprang to life with me in 2011, when I was taking stock of Tracking Wonder's audiences—readers, clients, participants, team members, social media followers—as a potentially cohesive group. "What held us together?" I wondered. "What could we name the people benefiting from Tracking

Wonder?" That same year, my Hudson Valley neighbor and wonder-tracking marketing maven Seth Godin published his influential book *Tribes: We Need You to Lead Us*. Godin defines a tribe as "a group of people connected to one another, connected to a leader, and connected to an idea." To step up for this growing, international, and—yes—mostly digital Tracking Wonder group, I needed to unite us with a term, but *tribe* didn't feel quite right.

I had recently grown interested in wolves after a few people commented that I had wolf energy—perhaps a kind of reflective leadership that came from spending time in solitude. I looked into the complex behaviors of wolf packs. I discovered, for instance, that in many cases, when a pack of wolves travels a long distance, they will keep pace with the slowest wolf in the pack. The more I read, the more I appreciated the emotional potential of calling our collective group of fans, followers, academy participants, lab attendees, team members, contributors, and clients a "pack."

I kept imagining how we might engage one another: a pack of wolves running wild together with the same collective intent, a shared mission to live creatively and with integrity. "Pack" stuck.

If you bristle at becoming part of a pack that might produce more groupthink than breakthroughs, remember that to be human is to be born into a pack. Your original family may not have nourished or inspired you the way you might have wanted, but you were born with the innate wiring to function in it. You can do so again, and on your terms. As a reformed introvert, I believe in the power of packs and have promoted this idea for over a decade. In at least three forms, packs can help you.

Support Packs

Does your dream need one or more people with a specific skill set you lack? If so, form a Support Pack that might include an assistant, editor, vendor, paid expert, consultant, freelancer, knowledge worker, employee, or contractor.

THE GENIUS OF SUPPORT PACKS

BETHANY HAMILTON
top performing surfer

By the time Bethany Hamilton was eight years old, her young genius showed itself on Maui's beaches. Compared to her older brothers, she seemed destined to soar as a surfer who one day could master the world's biggest waves, her dream from age eight on. And then at thirteen years old, Bethany was attacked. A one-ton, fourteen-foot tiger shark bit her board and her. Lucky to live, she escaped with her life and without her entire left arm. Aaron Lieber's documentary *Unstoppable* portrays Bethany's indomitable spirit. Family film footage captures bedridden Bethany, within days of the attack, smiling and looking soft-eyed into the camera, both grateful that the shark didn't attack her best friend and fully confident she would continue surfing. That young genius spirit led her—to the awe of friends, family, and competitors—not only to learn again how to surf but also to compete, to win more heats, and eventually to master twisting her board 360 degrees while surfing large waves.

But there's another angle to this story, one that seems to me the sub-story of *Unstoppable*. At every step of her life, Bethany had people recognizing, nourishing, and supporting her genius dream and drive. Her parents and best friend, the US Masters Swimmer swimming coach Dick Oliver, the ambulances at the ready, a water safety team leader who could steer her via a jet ski beyond the whitecap point and ride by her side, and the teachers and coaches throughout. Our genius can soar and ride seemingly insurmountable challenges when we are surrounded—or at least accompanied—by people who support our dream.

Nourish Packs

You inevitably need one or more people you can share your downers with so you can mend your wounds, alleviate worry, and move on constructively. A Nourish Pack might include one or more confidantes, a mentor or guide, close friends, or trusted family members.

THE GENIUS OF NOURISH PACKS

MINDY OHRINGER
novelist and creator of the Union & Utopia platform

What most impressed me when I first met and worked with Mindy Ohringer was her quick wit and indomitable prolific output. She can work on three interrelated novels simultaneously while publishing poems and short stories and earning writing residencies. Yet within two years of launching her platform Union & Utopia, her beloved husband of nearly forty years was diagnosed with advanced-stage pancreatic cancer. She, like many former clients, periodically updates me with message headlines such as "Days of Wonder, Sadness, and Howls at the Moon." She told me that a few things had kept her from losing faith. One important one that helped Mindy stay buoyant through her husband's worsening illness and eventual death was a pack of peers she had formed through Tracking Wonder. Each month over the years, this group has met online to share their work and encouragement. "Their love and support has lifted me up and kept me going," she wrote me. "Instead of feeling emotionally abandoned, I have experienced tremendous support and gained strength accordingly."

Wild Packs

Your dream likely needs perspective from other creative-minded people who have their own dream endeavors to pursue. A Wild Pack is your set of peers, a pack of fellow alpha wolves in parallel formation who mutually support and nudge one another forward.

THE GENIUS OF WILD PACKS

THE TRACKING WONDER INNER CIRCLE MASTERMIND

By the time the COVID-19 pandemic struck the globe in 2020 and forced every member of our Inner Circle MasterMind into lockdown, an interesting thing happened. Most of the group's participants, six able-minded people holding down responsibilities to family and (in some cases) teams while also advancing their dreams, said they felt prepared for the moment. Why was that? During the pandemic's initial brutal wave in spring 2020, one member said she felt ready because she had built the experimentation muscle, thanks largely to the Wild Pack's ability to keep seeing her at her best. Another member said that they each had modeled how to stay more curious and creative than fearful and fretful during personal challenges, and now this global challenge was a major test of those capacities. Our Wild Pack's social, emotional, and cognitive "net" gave them the brave space to continue testing out ideas and the freedom to be more of themselves as creative human beings.

Growth happens faster and deeper when we work well with others. DIT beats DIY.

A SPLASH OF HAPPINESS

Our older daughter can be moody, not unlike her papa. Our first morning of family vacation in the Adirondack Mountains a few years ago seemed no exception. This particular morning, I had risen at 5:30, meditated, journaled, and ran a mile down the road to discover a lake with cool morning mist rising off of it like mountain spirits waking up. I spontaneously turned off my runner's app, waltzed onto a wobbly dock, and sat and gazed at the rising mist for another five minutes. I then walked down another road, found a diner, ate a substantial breakfast, and walked back to our cabin.

I am not a regular runner, but this one summer, I finally discovered that elusive runner's flow that the author Haruki Murakami popularized in his book *What I Talk about When I Talk about Running*. On this morning, I felt wildly alive, and I was ready for the family to feel in co-flow. It's an alarming presumption: "If I'm in flow and ready to flow the whole day, well, why wouldn't you be?"

So I returned to the cabin with a coach's zeal and suggested that we go kayaking up Long Lake, a beautiful spindle of water tucked in the mountains. Everyone but my older daughter Dahlia seemed on board. As if I brought in a gust of cold wind instead of sunshine, a cloud formed over Dahlia's mood—impossible to determine why. If given her druthers, she'd rather read, write, and eat sweets all day than exert too much physical effort. At least, that's what she says. Yet once she's running or swimming or "Zumba-ing," the clouds vanish. Movement is a mood-changer. So I hedged my bets and nudged the family pack out the door. Dahlia slogged resentfully into a kayak with me.

We paddled along for about thirty minutes, our oars not necessarily in sync but still making our way up the lake. Almost stroke by stroke, she showed increasing curiosity. She wondered about the architecture of the homes we passed and who might live there. She noted the scent and height of the evergreens along the shore. How did the morning light create such alluring patterns on the water? Like the morning sky, she seemed to brighten up increasingly with every moment. Her spirit was waking up. Then we caught up with the other two and circled to head back home. A slight breeze picked up, which could have made the travel back difficult. Yet, for whatever reasons, she turned her head to the side to notice the rhythm of my oar paddling left, paddling right, paddling left, paddling right.

And without words, she matched my oar's rhythm and cadence with her own. *Left, right, left, right.* Something in my awareness shifted, and I felt calmly in harmony with the breeze rippling the waves and tossing refreshing drops onto our arms as we paddled in sync. It was as if for a moment we two partnered with the world around us. I had my iPad mini attached to a chest case and—never one to miss amping up a moment's bulb by a watt or two—I flipped on Mary Oliver's audiobook of poems from *At Blackwater Pond*. Right then, Oliver wonders aloud how there might be a single day "that doesn't have a splash of happiness."

A splash of happiness. Sometimes we expect that we will swim in an ocean of happiness in most endeavors and collaborations all day, every day. We expect that collaboration will feel like a well-practiced dance ensemble or a jazz masters' improv jam. No wonder we're disappointed. When we have unreal expectations, we miss the most real moments of joy, of openness, of harmony that can happen between two or more people, if only for a splash.

CONNECTION

Assess Your Bias Box

You can practice this invitation every day you encounter someone familiar or not—on a subway, in a grocery store, at the family dinner table. The technique for interrupting the adaptive unconscious that has worked for me and many of my clients is to ask more wondrous questions.

NOTICE WHEN YOU MEET SOMEONE FOR THE FIRST TIME. How did you, consciously or not, size up their personality, character, and worldview? If you meet them again, how can you give them a second chance by asking them more questions? What might their daily life be like? What do they dream about?

REFLECT ON A RECENT ENCOUNTER WITH SOMEONE YOU KNOW WELL. How have you assumed that this person would act, speak, or respond? How well did you really listen? When you see them next, how could you drop your assumptions and really listen, and even be surprised by what you hear?

Bust Your Bias Box

In all forms of potential collaboration and communication, you likely will find some or all these techniques helpful:

OBSERVE THE INVISIBLE ARMOR SIGNALS. You can feel *in your body* when your defenses start to rise. For me it comes with tight temples, neck, and shoulders. For you, just notice the next time you're in such a situation if you receive any somatic signals that your mind is closing.

OPEN UP; DON'T SIZE UP. Remember, our adaptive unconscious quickly "sizes up" people and ideas before giving them a chance. If you notice your cognitive armor rising, rub your temples. Stretch your neck. Connect with that part of you where the bias resides. Repeat this mantra to yourself over and over again: "Open up; don't size up."

LISTEN WITH YOUR FEET. When someone else is speaking, instead of focusing on what you're going to say next or trying to predict what that person is going to say, direct part of your awareness to your feet. By allocating part of your awareness in this way, you soften your attention's armor just a little more.

ASK QUESTIONS. If you're getting input that makes you uncomfortable or doesn't jibe with what you wanted, ask the person who offered the idea some questions. "What prompted that input?" or "Could you tell me more?" Be genuinely curious and seek understanding instead of coming out with your initial reaction.

Practice a Wonder Talk

Choose someone you trust to try this exercise with first. Then you can try it with someone you want to reestablish trust and deep connection with. Parents have tried it successfully with their children, siblings with each other, spouses with each other, and teammates with each other. The only supplies needed are a timer and possibly a box of tissues.

SIT FACING EACH OTHER WITH APPROXIMATELY ONE TO TWO FEET BETWEEN YOUR KNEES. Rest both feet flat on the ground, and both palms on your knees. Soften your jaw and your eyes. Decide who will be the speaker first and who will be the listener first. To make it simple, the person whose first name comes first in the English alphabet can be the first speaker.

TAKE A FEW MOMENTS TO CENTER IN THE SPACE BETWEEN YOU. Keep easeful eye contact as you direct your attention to your breath, evening the length of inhalations and exhalations. Then draw your attention to the space between you. Acknowledge that wonder is potentially a third party here.

REMEMBER A PLACE THAT BROUGHT YOU JOY. Draw your attention to your heart space. Eyes closed, bring to memory a place that has brought you great joy. It might be a vacation spot or a personal sanctuary from when you were a child or ten years ago, or it might be a place you visited just last week. Allow yourself to remember with your sensory imagination being there again. Observe what you see, hear, taste, smell, and feel. Open your eyes again.

LISTENER 1 PRACTICES TO THEMSELVES. Listener 1 will recall the two essential listener qualities, "Open up; don't size up" and "Listen with your feet."

SPEAKER 1 NOW HAS UP TO THREE MINUTES TO DESCRIBE THE JOYFUL PLACE. Use as much detail, imagery, and story as you want. The listener sits quietly and receives.

If any time remains, the listener does not relate their experience, analyze, or interpret. Instead, the listener asks questions to draw the speaker out even more. When complete, express appreciation to each other for holding the space. You might take a few moments to reflect to each other on how that experience felt to you.

Find a Pack

A **Nourish Pack** includes those people with whom you can each confide personal and professional struggles. Nourish Packs can be informal or formal, one-way or mutual. Let me explain. If you want one or more professionals you can lean on—a therapist, a coach—then you might create an informal pack in which *you* are the one receiving the emotional nourishment to advance your work. Most Nourish Packs, though, work best if you create a mutually nourishing "pact" for your pack.

MAKE A NOURISH PACK LIST. List the names of at least one other person you consider a confidante—someone in whom you can confide your emotional challenges and upsets as well as your hopes and aspirations as you advance your dream. Here are criteria to consider:

They listen well.

You trust them to hold confidentiality.

They are actively curious and keep an open, nonjudgmental mind.

A healthy **Support Pack** is right for you if your purpose for DIT is primarily to gather one or more talented people to keep your dream moving forward.

MAKE A SUPPORT PACK LIST. Write down the names of at least five core people who meet these criteria:

They believe in you and your dream.

They possess a skill set, area of expertise, or service that you do not, which will advance your dream.

They are willing to offer input on advancing your dream when asked.

They demonstrate active curiosity and a willingness to be open with others.

A **Wild Pack** is composed of a few trusted creatively minded people—not necessarily in your same field—who understand the vagaries of advancing complex dream endeavors every day because they are advancing their own. Everyone within a Wild Pack helps one another advance their dream endeavors with ongoing openness and curiosity as well as truthfulness and compassion.

MAKE A WILD PACK LIST. List at least three people you know who also are pursuing their own endeavors—whether it's a business, a creative project, a startup project, a side gig, or all of these. The aim here is to meet on a regularly scheduled basis to share parts of your endeavors and to receive input or encouragement. Here are criteria to consider:

They have a conscious bias toward taking experimental action.

They possess a healthy other-centeredness.

They are capable of understanding the complex decisions you must make and steps you must take to experiment with your dream.

They are curious, open-minded, and listen well.

They are capable of being responsible to meeting regularly with the Wild Pack.

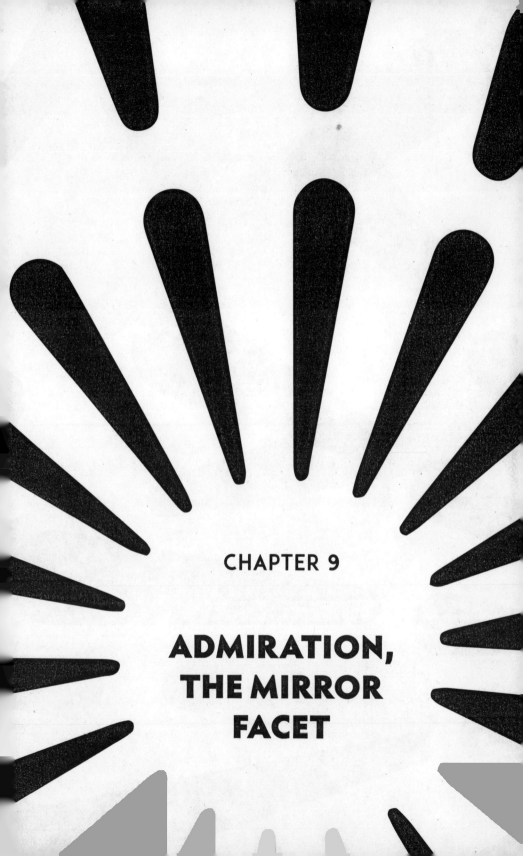

CHAPTER 9

ADMIRATION, THE MIRROR FACET

LIKE MOST KIDS, I wanted to fit in with my peers, but I usually bucked against simple conformity. By age six, I grew my hair long in the '70s way before it was fashionable, and when I enrolled in judo classes that required an all-white uniform, I spent more time pretending I was Elvis than flipping kids on the mat. I knew I didn't want to emulate my parents' lifestyle, but what my life would be like, I had no idea.

By age thirteen, I spent my late Saturday nights with John Belushi, Gilda Radner, and the rest of the *Saturday Night Live* crew. My parents, who would divorce later that year, often stayed out late with their friends and left me to my own devices. If I wasn't sneaking off to some adolescent party or to toilet-paper a neighbor's trees, I was reading stories, watching television, and listening to music. SNL combined my passions (without the toilet paper), along with an edgy, witty point of view I relished. Nothing was sacred or above being mocked.

One night, David Bowie was the guest artist for what became one of the most memorable episodes for me and much of America. The artist had completely transformed himself from his red-headed Ziggy Stardust alter ego and looked equally different from his quite mainstream appearance years earlier on *Bing Crosby's Merrie Olde Christmas* special. (I would find out years later that the producers pleaded with Bowie backstage to remove his lipstick and earrings for that family show.) On SNL, over three different musical numbers, Bowie showcased his edgy pop sensibility, jumping in and out of unexpected costumes. Flanked by two other avant-garde performers, he first stuffed himself into a giant plastic tuxedo, then dressed like a Chinese stewardess, and finally came out as a marionette, complete with remotely operated arms. His ability to shape-shift into different identities held me spellbound. Here was a grown man whose clean face and groomed blond haircut looked like that of my friends, and somehow he could dress and perform in outrageous attire while standing in full confidence of his vocal range and songwriting virtuosity.

Who was this man who could captivate his audience so confidently and powerfully? And what did he mean to my young self?

It was reported that when Bowie starred in the film *The Man Who Fell to Earth*, he brought a trunk with fifteen hundred books with him to read during breaks—books that ranged from obscure fiction and the occult to philosophy and animal behavior. Later, music critics would attest that Bowie's diverse interests regularly fed his innovations and the multiple iterations he went through with his identity. He fluidly crossed binary borders of gender and refused easy artistic categorization. He could be at home hanging out with punk icon Iggy Pop and Hollywood star Elizabeth Taylor in the same week. On that one Saturday night when his glamorous image was projected across the nation, I was utterly fascinated, even enchanted. Bowie didn't just fascinate me, though; I came to admire him. To admire someone, it turns out, is a wholly different experience, one rich with wonder.

FACET 6: ADMIRATION

Admiration often occurs in unexpected moments between two or more people. Psychologists Sara B. Algoe and Dacher Keltner, who have studied admiration's relationship to excellence, note that the *Oxford English Dictionary* defines *admiration* as "agreeable surprise; wonder mingled with reverence, esteem, approbation," a definition likely influenced by Charles Darwin's impression that admiration is "surprise associated with some pleasure and a sense of approval."

Admiration, we could say, is to experience a surprising love for someone else's excellence that can awaken us to become better at what we do and how we do it. In Bowie, I saw the possibility that grown-up life could become an endless quest for creative reinvention. That promise of creative courage stood in stark contrast to the model I saw all around me, where adults held jobs to pay the bills, raised a family, partied on the weekends, and washed up to go to church on Sunday mornings. Others similarly recognized the escape from conformity that Bowie offered. The English philosopher Simon Critchley writes, "Just as Bowie seemingly reinvented himself without limits, he allowed us to believe that our capacity for changes was limitless." (*Ch-ch-ch changes!* was a personal anthem.) This multifaceted artist showed us that we could keep pursuing our quirky curiosities in a way that also created moving experiences for others. I have realized that fostering admiration is a hidden talent, a virtue of generosity among many exemplary as well as everyday geniuses of creativity.

Admiration, we could say, is to experience a surprising love for someone else's excellence that can awaken us to become better at what we do and how we do it.

Here's a notable discovery about the English word *admiration*'s roots: The Latin *mira* means "wonder." From *mira* the English language also gives us the word *mirror*. In admiration, wonder happens between us. We watch another person adeptly lead a team through crisis with grace, or we observe musicians deftly convert their interests into their dazzling creative work, or we read the sentences of a novelist that spin our imaginations in tantalizing ways. When we actively observe people doing what they do exceptionally well, they can connect us to a set of deeply held ideals and values that we could live out in our own way. We also can be admired, too, as we become mirrors of possibility to the people who could benefit from the fruits of our work. Admiration, it turns out, is a wonder mirror.

Like the facet of connection, the facet of admiration can redirect your attention outward toward other people—again, both in admiring them and in engendering their admiration.

How can we foster this reflective facet of wonder without slipping into admiration's traps of envy, inadequacy, or deference? Let's see what's possible.

ADMIRE INSTEAD OF DEFER

Admiration is not deference. I suspect this slippery trap is one reason some of us skeptics flinch even at the sound of "admiring" another human being. My Zen teacher John Daido Loori once said, "If you walk into a room and smell a guru, run." My yoga teacher Sri T. K. V. Desikachar chose early on not to go the path of the guru but the path of the venerable teacher (acharya). So, your fostering a healthy admiration of another person whose skill and character uplift your own potential is notably different from an unhealthy veneration of an idol that diminishes your potential in deference to an authority. Let's be aware of the difference.

We can, however, practice this "other-praising" emotion in a way that inspires us to improve what we do and how. Through a series of studies, the psychologists Jonathan Haidt of New York University Stern School of Business and Sara B. Algoe of the University of North Carolina at Chapel Hill set out to examine that correlation. As they note, "People are often profoundly moved by leaders, saints, benefactors, and heroes, as well as by ordinary people who do extraordinary things"—people they call "exemplary others."

Haidt and Algoe note that we are moved to excel by witnessing other human beings principally in two ways: by admiring someone's exceptional skill, achievement, and talent (admiration) and by witnessing someone else's exceptional virtue (elevation). Admiration gives us the "chills," one of the studies showed. It does so more than joy or even elevation. That fact surprised the scientists. Moments of joy and amusement bring us pleasure but they don't light us up to get better at what we do and how. Moments of admiration energized participants most strongly to improve themselves, advance their skills and talents, and reach their own goals. In other words, admiration inspired them to excel and fulfill their potential.

Experiencing—and *practicing*—admiration also could alter the way we view other people. Those people who experienced admiration or elevation were more likely to have a renewed view or respect toward the other person being observed than those people who experienced joy—who tended to focus much more on their own experiences instead of on other people. Haidt and Algoe also note that "admiration seems to make people want to tell others how great the person was, thereby potentially enhancing the person's reputation." Simply put, having experiences of elevation, gratitude, and admiration "draws people out of themselves."

If a person is someone you have turned your admiration toward often, we might call that person a paragon or exemplar—someone whom you regard as a model of excellence in a certain way. Note that your viewing such a person as a paragon does not mean that you regard that person as "perfect" in some unrealistic fashion, nor does it mean that you worship this person, as it were, without question.

There's another potential pitfall here, though. After all, some participants in the Haidt and Algoe studies watched Michael Jordan glide, twist, and swoosh across courts and felt more humbled than inspired to excel. What's the line between admiring someone who uplifts you and comparing-and-despairing? And what happens when we feel more envy than admiration?

THE SURPRISING ADVANTAGE OF ENVY

Those of us prone to feel admiration are also susceptible to envy, which can lead to sadness, fear, or shame. Admiration feels good, but envy feels bad. Akin to admiration, envy is the negative aspect of how we might initially respond to another's superior skills, accomplishments, or status. Envy occurs when you compare yourself to someone else whom you believe has a superior quality, skill, or achievement, and you subsequently find yourself lacking. It can be a classic case of compare-and-despair.

I've worked with many otherwise accomplished people who feel the "green with envy" wave. If you've spent any time online, you know what I'm talking about. You see someone who from the outside seems to do what they do so exceptionally well. They're making spectacular contributions to the world. Everything in life and work seems to go their way.

Yet not all envy is the same. If we experience malicious envy, we secretly hope for, if not gloat about, the other person's failure (*schadenfreude*)—especially that seemingly all-too-perfect person online. For our purposes, though, the concept of "benign envy" could help us understand how to harness admiration of others for our personal and creative growth. Benign envy is when someone else spurs feelings of diminished worth in us and yet we respond by wanting to achieve at a higher level. The response is not to outdo the other person as much as rise to our own potential.

In 2011, the Dutch psychologist Niels van de Ven and his team tested the effects of benign envy. Their research questions were inspired by the Danish philosopher Søren Kierkegaard, who wrote in *The Sickness Unto Death* that while "admiration is happy self-surrender . . . envy is unhappy self-assertion." In van de Ven's experiment, college students read fake biographies of made-up scientists. One passage was embedded with the principle that hard work leads to success. The second passage described success as completely due to luck. Then the students all read a fake newspaper account of a college student who had won an impressive competition.

The results showed that if the participants were primed with the idea of success requiring hard work, they felt some benign envy toward the winner. Those influenced by the idea that success is due to luck merely admired the winner. Then both sets of students were asked to pledge an amount of hours they would study that term.

Which group wanted to study more? The ones who felt benign envy. In a follow-up study, van de Ven found that students under the spell of benign envy achieved better results on an assessment of their creativity than did students feeling only admiration. From these and other studies, it appears that benign envy could play a role in activating self-improvement.

You can track admiration or even benign envy in a healthy way—and you can witness when those all-too-common feelings of compare-and-despair arise. Let me share a personal squirmy example.

I often want to be a better papa. I view anything I seriously want to be better at, including papahood, as a practice if not a craft. I can get myself into trouble, though, if I start comparing myself to how some of my friends and colleagues "appear" online as fathers. One of my acquaintances is a psychologist, author of multiple engaging books, a professor, and an ultra-loving and adventurous dad to three girls. He's younger and profoundly "buffer" than I am; he seems equally as productive, if not more so, than me; and for years he has posted photographs of him and his girls eating triple-stack pancakes, leaping off cliffs into lakes, piloting airplanes, and, well, you get the picture. My first reaction, after getting over my jealousy of his bulging biceps and my benign envy of his gung-ho spirit, is, "I want to be a father like that!" Then I have to ask myself what I mean by "that."

What is the "that" that I seemingly want to be? Pause. This pause to ask and define a response to this question is essential. If I don't take this next step, then I could just stew in feelings of inadequacy as I scroll my social media feed and then see my girls that evening. In this case, it's not that I want to imitate exactly the *things* he does with his girls. It's more his presence, his joy, and his intentional aim to bolster his daughters' courage that I *admire* and desire to *emulate*, not imitate.

So before my downer mind starts comparing my quiet and older Atticus Finch to his vibrant daredevil Captain Fantastic, I pause again. I acknowledge how I can actually make even more time to create courage-boosting and skill-building explorations with my girls—all in ways that suit *my* nature and that of *my* two girls in my one life. I know I practice being emotionally attuned to both girls, but watching my friend in turn inspired something more in my abilities as a father. This last step helps me see myself and my core genius in a healthy self-regard. In a non-smarmy way, I get a dose of self-admiration that boosts my immunity to a viral case of compare-and-despair. I can move forward with a healthy, action-inspiring admiration. Watching my friend's way of fatherhood has inspired me to get my girls on horses, swim in meets, climb more trees, wrestle, play piano, and more.

There's also another mindset shift you can practice when observing other people's virtuosity in ways you want to excel at. You can actively take pleasure in observing your peers' displays of exceptional craft or character. The psychologists Jonathan Haidt and Dacher Keltner coined this form of appreciation as *tugendfreude*—the opposite of wishing for their failure, schadenfreude. So the next time envy arises in such a moment, try to appreciate precisely what the other person does well or the ideal you value that the other person exhibits.

Make admiration a practice and you more likely avoid those unconscious pitfalls of deference, self-sabotaging comparison, or malicious envy.

LISTEN, YOU A WONDER

The accomplished poet Lucille Clifton knew this fine line between admiration and envy. When Clifton visited her husband at Harvard, where he taught in the 1970s, she noticed how all the female students looked heart-achingly youthful, thin, and vibrant. Some sensation of envy must have overcome her. She said that she felt out of place among these girls and, for a moment, questioned her worth, which seems preposterous to people familiar with this audaciously eloquent, full-bodied, and radiant Black artist. Clifton had raised six children—at one point, all of them were under seven. Yet she had prevailed to further her own life as a poet whose first collection, *Good Times*, was published in 1969. The *New York Times* named it one of the top ten books of the year. By this time, Clifton had been a poet in residence at Coppin State College in Baltimore, and in the years to come, she would serve as Maryland's poet laureate and would go on to teach at University of California, Santa Cruz, St. Mary's College of Maryland, and Columbia University. Yet here she was on Harvard's campus feeling diminished, not because of her accomplishments but most likely because of her outward appearance, one that she had previously praised as "mighty" and "magic" in her empowering poem "homage to my hips."

So what do you do when you get self-conscious about how other people might see you and judge you? When you feel other people aren't really seeing the best in you? When you feel you don't belong in their beautiful-people club? I, for one, despite whatever outward accomplishments I've achieved, might shrink and try to disappear. Clifton didn't shrink. She created. That night she went to her room and she wrote a poem that portrayed her body and her soul with open eyes. In the poem "what the mirror said," she imagines standing before a mirror that speaks right back to her. It begins this way:

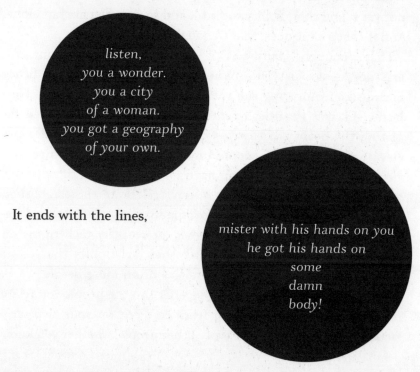

listen,
you a wonder.
you a city
of a woman.
you got a geography
of your own.

It ends with the lines,

mister with his hands on you
he got his hands on
some
damn
body!

"Some damn body." That was who Clifton affirms—not only for herself but also for anyone reading the poem who ever felt self-conscious about their appearance. The poem asks how we can hold ourselves and one another in high regard for the rich mysteries we are. In this case, the mirror is not a tool of vanity reflecting obsessive self-love. No, just as the literal mirror reflected her exquisite depths that perhaps the svelte eighteen-year-olds had not yet gained, this poem acts as a mirror that reflects our wondrous complexities.

Here's what I admire about Clifton's creative response. She gives herself a healthy dose of self-admiration and then creates a poem that in turn acts like such a mirror to others. Clifton's body—of writing and more—does for her readers what your gesture, work, or endeavor might do for the people you want to touch and uplift. Many of her poems memorialized and deeply described the experiences of African ancestors and other figures who might not be able to speak for themselves—people who are not the typical "heroes" celebrated in conventional history books and speeches. What poetry can do, Clifton says, is "speak for those who have not yet found their ability to speak and to say, 'You are not alone.' And if that's all it does, that's enough."

That's enough. Many artists—painters, musicians, songwriters, poets—do just this. Whether it's the songwriter Bruce Springsteen capturing the voice of a working-class guy in New Jersey, or the twentieth-century painter Jacob Lawrence depicting the beauty of laboring people, these creative endeavors elevate the beauty of people in their everyday hardships and victories. This kind of art can have a subtle effect on how we see ourselves and one another. It doesn't celebrate the established heroes: military generals, high-profile martyrs of traditional history, Olympic athletes, slim models, or wealthy tech titans on business magazine covers. Instead, their art uplifts the accomplishments of the overlooked, who are often more heroic.

You can have a similarly uplifting effect on the people you relate to. You might realize that your work isn't just for your own satisfaction. Your actions could elevate other people, whether you know it or not. Why not consider that possibility, and why not wake up tomorrow morning, ready to play just a little better for the people who might benefit from your work? You a wonder, indeed.

ADMIRE THE ADMIRERS

How, then, could other people's admiration of your work affect both your creative output and the influence you have on others? Does it matter if you lock yourself up in your creative cave and disregard the rest of humanity? There is wisdom in not allowing others' opinions of you to determine your self-worth (as Lucille Clifton's poem echoes), but could your work or realized dream have more influence if you practice shifting your attention toward other people and foster admiring relationships?

Dean Keith Simonton, the author of *Origins of Genius*, set out to find out. For the study "Artistic Creativity and Interpersonal Relationships Across and Within Generations," Simonton identified eleven kinds of relationships eminent artists are likely to have. Through Simonton's complex formula that examined the biographical data on 772 artists, his study showed that family relationships might not be as influential as previously thought by psychologists believing the theory that creative genius is largely hereditary. "It seems that artistic talent," he wrote, "does not run in families—only mediocrity does." Which relationships do have positive effects? Connections of admiration, which include the number of people the artist admired as paragons of excellence as well as the number of people who, in turn, admired the artist. Simonton's study highlights the important reciprocity of directing your admiration toward others and receiving it from them, too. Even if you have no aspirations to become a famous artist, certain relationships of admiration might propel your endeavor forward and outward in ways you could not imagine. This small shift in perspective could have big ripples of impact.

Wonder, remember, acts like a reset button that helps us see again what is real and true, beautiful and possible. For a moment, our default biases dissolve. Such moments can happen with a slight reframing of the people who could benefit from your work, your actions, or your skills development. These people might be your coworkers or teammates, your children or other family members, your customers or clients, your readers or audience members. You can make this shift toward admiration if you imagine these people as everyday heroes.

I have observed that everyday geniuses of creativity of many stripes possess a healthy regard for the people who they can influence for the better as potential heroes of sorts. For example, the writer John Green has published five bestselling YA novels and has Twitter followers in the millions. It's not just his exceptional craft that leads to his wide-ranging positive influence. He also greatly respects and admires his readers—namely, the thirteen-to-nineteen-year-old set. "I'm tired of adults telling teenagers they're not smart," he told an adolescent reporter for *The Guardian*.

Admiration happens both ways, then. One of my clients, Millie, is senior associate dean for research for a major university's library systems. During the 2020–2021 COVID-19 pandemic, the faculty was in frequent turmoil and distress. That year she and her boss also often didn't see eye to eye, and she felt disrespected as he kept lengthening her already long list of job responsibilities. Unknown to most faculty, though, Millie also had extensive training in restorative yoga and mindfulness meditation. So she started offering faculty online sessions she called "Release and Restore" that included relaxing breathwork, meditation, and journaling. At first, holding these sessions seemed risky because they were not typical "academic" fare, and Millie had never really shown this side to her peers. But she started actively appreciating these faculty and seeing how hard some of them worked despite the constant challenges and changes they had faced that year. That shift in how she regarded them motivated her to take a chance. It turns out that most of the faculty loved these sessions and appreciated this newly discovered part of their associate dean.

One day Millie expressed to me, "I had a breakthrough with my boss." Everyone seemed distressed again at the prospect of returning to campus during a time when cases of COVID-19 were unpredictable. During an online meeting to discuss the return to campus, the dean said, "Well, I asked myself, 'What would Millie do?' Breathe. So, that's what I've been doing more of. Breathing." When I asked her how that felt when he said that, she said, "I felt seen. And I feel motivated to keep holding the sessions."

Admiration from peers can make us truly happy, more so than wealth or economic status. That is one conclusion from a study by Berkeley researchers. The researchers, including Dacher Keltner, propose that more than socioeconomic status, the factors that contribute to people's well-being are their peers' respect and admiration—what the scientists call a "local ladder effect."

Imagine two lit-up mirrors facing each other and reflecting the best in each other. Imagine the infinite ripples of that kind of genuine positive reflection.

Everyday heroes are people who desire change, big or small, permanent or temporary. Many of them, like you, view life as a quest inherent with discovery, surprise, and challenge—and they might meet and surmount those challenges often with a quiet courage. They might be open to changing their views on a topic you care about. Maybe they seek to improve their quality of life or work, or enact a change in fortune or health. Everyday heroes could be people who read your blog or listen to your podcast, who come to your restaurant or your retreat, who buy your book or your card decks, who download your app or use your car wash. Fulfilling your dream can ignite such a meaningful moment of change for them. This shift in regard for the people whom you serve can expand your outlook and elevate your spirit to show up for them in a new way.

This reframe scales broadly. When a large city's planning department hired me to help design and communicate a multi-year process for their first-ever comprehensive city plan, I kept hearing a misaligned focus. The city faced a dire situation. The population had soared in recent years. Foreign investment and other factors contributed to a widening chasm between the haves and have-nots. The city was quickly becoming unaffordable, and despite their city often being regarded as one of the planet's most naturally beautiful and prosperous places, they weren't prepared for the coming impact of climate change. The department's team imagined a future that would make the city sustainable for everyone: its impoverished and marginalized residents, the wealthy communities, and the prosperous business and tech sectors. To the department's credit, we quickly agreed that we would develop a yearlong visioning process that would enlist the collaboration of citizens—as opposed to the old model of the department developing a plan and imposing it on the residents.

I picked up on a key tension. On one hand, I heard from certain team members a desire not unlike Lucille Clifton's expression of what poetry can do. They wanted to give voice to the voiceless: indigenous people, non-English speaking immigrant populations, youth. In the first session, though, I kept hearing subtle disparagements toward the city dwellers who were financially comfortable and might resist any change because they wanted to protect their neighborhoods' property values. Yet these were the very people they knew they had to enlist as part of the planning process. This tension is common. Businesses, for instance, want to serve people, yet those people often are viewed as inconveniences, irritations, or abstract transactions.

I suggested to the city planning department that we instead identify segments of the city population as heroes. Many team members seemed surprised by the use of the word *hero*. Why *wouldn't* they balk? After all, if you've ever attended a city council or local planning board meeting, it's hard to imagine the people yelling at city representatives as "heroes." But this framing would be private among the department, designed to help us gain a new appreciation for the concerns, frustrations, and challenges that even these more privileged populations face. This way we would be in a much healthier position for the department to listen to and engage their participation.

It was a stretch for some team members at first to even imagine certain privileged citizens' desires with much respect, yet they understood that if their city plan were to result in a resilient, healthy, vibrant, and sustainable place for citizens for several generations, then they needed a shift in their attitude toward *all* stakeholders. While it took some time, that transformation helped their leader and other members carry out a series of conversations, meetings, and creative ways to enlist all citizens' input. In the initial phase, they gathered responses from over nine thousand people to over fifty thousand questions in five languages.

Fostering admiration for citizens positively influenced the design. It helped this city department execute a collaborative approach with citizen-heroes. As their mindset shifted toward admiring these different citizen segments, the city government in many respects earned those citizens' respect and admiration as well.

Hero engagement is a model in which everyone on both sides of the exchange is elevated. Create admiration toward "your people," and the wonder of being human together infuses the work.

RECEIVE APPRECIATION, NOT ADULATION

Remember how admiration is most effective when it's reciprocal? Yet many of us are uncomfortable accepting positive feedback and appreciation. We have ingrained beliefs against projecting any nuance of self-satisfaction in our responses, and we frequently feel imposter syndrome. If we discount or brush off the admiration that people want to show us, we're not helping them.

Yet to accept tributes to yourself, whether for your innate qualities or your work, allows other people to receive the benefits of the admiration they give. If you're not accustomed to gracefully accepting praise, that's a good skill to work on. When you receive appreciation, refrain from quickly deflecting attention back to the other person or deprecating your talents. A gracious, genuine "Thank you" often suffices. Doing so could increase your own happiness and fulfillment.

But beware of seeking adulation instead of earning admiration. If you become public with your work, or if people at your office start to recognize your efforts, you could stay stuck. The actor gets addicted to applause, the teacher to praise, the artist to adulation, the online influencer to social media's likes.

Applause, praise, adulation—it all seems like innocuous good feedback. We're doing good, apparently. We're making a difference. Bringing joy. Why can't we bask in that? Well, we can, of course. The trap is when we get stuck in the basking and can't see our way past the praise. The trap is when the desire for applause is what drives us and feeds us.

What I'm getting at here involves the more nuanced social dynamic between you and the people who receive your work. If you mostly seek their adoration, then you do little to inspire their own potential greatness. You also forfeit your own opportunity to expand your awareness and sense of self toward others.

Instead, show up for the work you and your genius are here for. Live this one life each day like the symphony you're here to make. Play it well at your best. Then in your natural way, redirect the light to shine on others.

When you do so, love can glow infinitely on the net that connects us all.

ADMIRATION

Track Your Admiration

Whom have you looked toward with admiration? It might
be a teacher who at once was knowledgeable, adept at their
skill, and inspiring. Possibly it's someone who has excelled
in your field of work. Maybe it's even someone you have
watched from afar, whose work and life have inspired you
to be a better version of you or to get better at how you do
what you do in your way.

In your Tracking Wonder notebook, recall and write into
a specific time that gave you a positive feeling when you
observed this person in action or learned about something
they did.

Explore this question: What *one quality* or *one action* do
you especially admire in them that *could be* a reflection of
what's possible in you?

Explore the possibility that the uplift you feel when admiring this person could reflect that something within you
feels called to rise, so to speak. In this way, you turn the
mirror back on your genius.

Your writing for a few minutes in this way makes admiration more personable and real to you. It also *extends*
admiration's ripple effect on you.

Turn Benign Envy into Creative Admiration

There are four ways to work with benign envy I've found effective within our community.

IDENTIFY THE "THAT." Remember that father I envied and said to myself, "I want to be like that?" When you catch yourself thinking in this potentially downer pattern, identify the "that." Then turn the mirror back to yourself and own up to what you already have within you to be more of your genius self instead of trying to be more like someone else.

START A FIELD STUDY. When clients venture into new territory in their endeavors, feelings of envy and even compare-and-despair often arise. So rather than bypass those feelings, we do what I did when I first ventured Tracking Wonder into the public as a business and project—conduct a field study. To do so, create a simple field study document or section in your Tracking Wonder notebook. List three to five people who work within your field whom you admire. They might be your peers. Make it a regular practice to observe what you specifically admire about what they do—but then aspire not to imitate them but to emulate their actions or qualities. Reflect back on you and your genius. In my early twenties, for instance, as I was first deliberately honing my writing craft, I read Annie Dillard's Pulitzer Prize–winning nonfiction book *Pilgrim at Tinker Creek* that she had written when she was twenty-nine. Something in her exquisite sentences, sneaky metaphors, smooth research, and poignant observations about the nature of seeing made my head twist. For most of that year I kept a "Sentence Notebook," a notebook devoted to my copying down verbatim those mind-blowing sentences. I became a student of sentences, and Dillard became my remote mentor.

PRACTICE TUGENDFREUDE. Remember, that's the coined phrase by two psychologists for how you can practice feeling pleasure and joy—along with benign envy—upon learning of or observing someone's achievement or excellence. Even extend them a note of congratulations or appreciation.

ABSORB APPRECIATION. Think back to specific praise or appreciation you have received in a relevant area. If the feedback was written, reread it. What did this person see in you uniquely? Maybe it was a teacher who recognized your talent for dancing or your talent for humor. Maybe a colleague saw your genius for bringing people together for a common cause. In those moments, something opens within us. Absorb how that appreciation resonates within you. Let it affect you and motivate you.

A marvelous and devoted professor I knew once told me in his office that when he gets down on himself or hears un-warranted criticism, he goes to his "Real Paycheck Drawer." He pulled open a side drawer from his desk. In it were stacks of cards and lengthy letters that students had writ-ten him—sometimes ten or more years after taking a course with him—that told him what his fervor for teaching meant to them and how it changed their lives in so many ways. "That's my real paycheck, Jeffrey," he said.

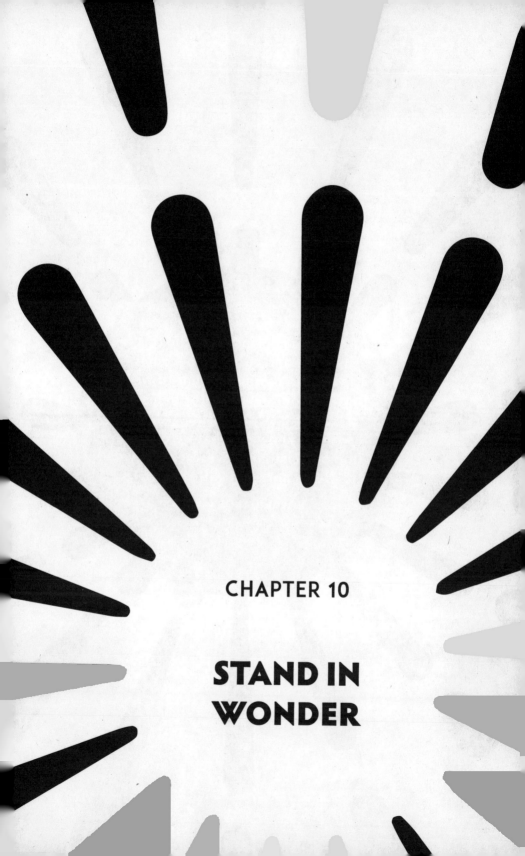

CHAPTER 10

STAND IN
WONDER

What begins in childlike wonder and curiosity becomes, with the passage of time, if we persist in our devotion (or delusion), a "calling"; a "profession." Almost without knowing what we do, we find ourselves in places we've never been, nor even anticipated.

JOYCE CAROL OATES
prolific author of over one hundred books

WE DON'T NEED PERMISSION to be what we innately are: wondrous. Yet it feels that way sometimes. The truth is that many members of our community have confided that these practices have given them confidence and courage to stand in wonder.

Stand in wonder? How do we stand in something so ephemeral and fleeting? That's been an ongoing question for me and the people in our community since I was visited by the yellow monarch. Throughout this book, I've invited you to track each facet of wonder in the exercise section of each chapter. Thank you for taking this tracking wonder journey with me so far. It has been a profound gift to receive, and then transmit to others, this understanding of how wonder operates.

In this chapter, you'll journey through a set of frameworks and invitations designed to embolden your commitment to leading a wondrous life of creative purpose. It's my intent that you will come back to this chapter—and in fact specific chapters from this book—as you advance toward different stages on your journey.

STAND IN DEVOTION

When in college, I discovered the existentialist psychologist Erich Fromm's *The Art of Loving*. In this elegant slim volume, Fromm observes how we become fixated on falling in love and being loved. But he says love—or more precisely, loving another—is an art that requires a deepening knowledge and persistent effort. When you love artfully, you're not motivated by fleeting passions nor to alleviate your own loneliness but by an intentional drive to love *better*. Love, he writes, "is a 'standing in,' not a 'falling for.'" That phrase "standing in" has stuck with me ever since. To stand in love fosters an abiding, mature dedication. It took me many more years and trial relationships to embody the art of loving—and I'm still practicing it.

And many years later, my experience and research offered this insight: A similar principle is true of committing to a specific endeavor or a creative life in general. It's one thing to fall in love with a fantasy you've conjured. It's another more abiding thing to stand in wonder with a dream you're devoted to.

Devotion. It's an appropriate word for what's required to cross the threshold from witnessing fleeting moments of wonder to standing in wonder. Devotion reaches more deeply than short-lived passion; it does not flee challenges but instead meets them as opportunities to go deeper.

Your devotion reminds you in a visceral way why you're pursuing what you're pursuing. Devotion, which heeds that deep calling, imbues your actions with an expansive intention and spirit. Gandhi knew something about right action in the face of seemingly insurmountable challenges. "Without devotion," he writes, "action and knowledge are cold and dry, and may even become shackles." Devoted action, on the other hand, perhaps can liberate you not only from doubt but also from self-centeredness.

Invitation: Stand in Devotion

I invite you to adjust your posture so you feel in your body a sense of dignity and stability. Let the volume and pace of your breathing be full yet easeful.

To help your conscious mind anchor its attention, you may place your right hand on your heart space and your left on your lower belly. Bring awareness to the placement of your two hands—the heart pulsing with the intelligence of life plus the intelligence of the gut.

Now bring to your awareness the feeling of *you* rising every day to stand in wonder with your deepest dream. Absorb for a moment the emotions and qualities you are devoted to bringing forward through your endeavors and work. Are you devoted to bringing forward more courage? More equity? More creativity? Is there an intention to bring forward more healthy change for other people or for a whole community? To bring beauty and joy to your family or an aging parent or students? To bring peace and well-being to health-care workers?

Now ask your whole self this question: "What am I devoted to?"

Observe what word or phrase or image registers a deep wholehearted response in you. Imagine that response circulating through your heart, traversing through your blood, and traveling through your gut so that your devotion informs much of your intentional actions and decisions this very day. Observe how that feels.

I encourage you to write down in your Tracking Wonder notebook what word, phrase, statement, or image arose. Tag it as your devotion for now, and for the next few days keep coming back to this practice to remind yourself of your devotion. This way you can operate at a level beyond being mired in conflict, disappointment, or emotional reactivity.

DEFINE YOUR DREAM ENDEAVOR

Perhaps a moment of wonder has sparked a sense of purpose for you in the past. Lee Rankin's momentary glimpse into the eyes of an alpaca gave her a mission that she pursued with dogged determination. Many driven people describe how they "knew in an instant" that something grand had begun in their lives after witnessing wonder. Then they took steps to implement the insight. If you are primed to pay attention to wonder, you'll heed the call of the inspiration and understand the need for acting on it.

You might recall how you reacted to an uncanny coincidence, remember a moment of deep connection with someone, or flip through a photo album to spark once again the motivating feelings of wonder. Note that sometimes purpose comes from pain. A client of mine described how in the depths of despair after a breakup, she realized she was called to help women feel empowered in relationships. She went on to launch a program that now serves thousands of participants.

Try not to think of purpose as some unattainable ideal. Purpose can arise in everyday contexts: a mom caring for her child, a musician performing original songs, or a lawyer arguing in court. To carry out purpose, create the conditions for accomplishing something meaningful to you that also has a positive impact on others. In my work, I call this a "dream endeavor."

If you are primed to pay attention to wonder, you'll heed the call of the inspiration and understand the need for acting on it.

A dream endeavor is any initiative, project, or venture that puts your dreams for a better life or better world in motion. Your dream endeavor does not have to fit into any kind of professional category. If your screenplay could entertain other people while bringing out your storytelling talents, then that screenplay is your dream endeavor. Renovating your house for your growing family's daily life is a dream endeavor. Starting a new school program or fostering rescue animals is a dream endeavor. If you look around, dream endeavors are the common denominator among people leading their most fulfilling lives.

A dream endeavor often will stretch you beyond your comfort zone, demanding a lot of you psychologically and emotionally. To keep the dream in motion, you'll meet a series of challenges and need to work with one or more people. You might be tempted to shut down, overreact, or throw in the towel of self-defeat. But for these reasons and more, wonder can be a versatile ally and a surprising advantage.

Imogen Daly is a wildlife biologist whose engagement with wonder allowed her to embrace the power of her work and share it more readily with others. She is involved with protecting the habitat of the desert tortoise, which lives in remote and rugged areas of the Sonoran and Mojave deserts. She has assisted with the five largest translocations of any species in the United States, moving thousands of animals to new locations out of harm's way.

"Wonder and flow in the desert tortoise habitat are very much a part of the way I move and experience being there, and why I continue this work," Daly said. "The environment is so raw, expansive, elegant, and resilient, and being so intimate with an ancient species fills me with wonder." Imogen described being in the presence of a magical, ancient tortoise as being like sitting with her great-grandmother, her guide and teacher of the land. Witnessing the pace at which tortoises move taught Daly patience, presence, and the power of observation. "Being in wonder with these animals allows a greater sense of just being in the moment. I experience wonder as the whisper of the natural world, and when I hear it, I relax and have a feeling of coming home and being connected to all that is around me."

Working with the exercises of tracking wonder allowed Daly a safe environment to experience the joy of her feelings about her work. She reported being much freer of self-doubt than before. "I now feel I understand how to walk in alignment with my purpose, and I can participate in the world more fully," she said.

Daly stands in wonder by writing every day and finding ways to use her voice. "In a time with such tragic effects of climate change, sharing my love of the natural world with others helps me do my part," she stated. Imogen found her purpose and now gifts wonder every day.

Now, what is *your* dream endeavor?

Invitation: The Three Questions

You may adjust your posture so you feel in your body a sense of dignity and stability. Let the volume and pace of your breathing be full yet easeful as you consider these questions:

THE POSSIBILITY QUESTION: What work, project, or activity most lights you up with possibility? Maybe there's a word or image that arises. If so, notice how it feels to focus on it.

THE IMPACT QUESTION: What work, project, or activity potentially could make a big difference in the lives of people you care about engaging? Again, a word or image might arise. If so, observe how that feels.

THE GENIUS QUESTION: What work, project, or activity could most bring out the strengths, skills, or young genius traits you uniquely possess that you want to bring forward? If a word or image arises, observe how it feels.

In your Tracking Wonder notebook, write into the possibility of what you and only you—or possibly your team or organization—can contribute to the world. That answer might change a lot over the course of your life as you respond at different times to what calls you.

DEFLECT DETRACTORS

Beware the detractors: The seed of your dream can be crushed before it even has a chance to sprout. That's why in the early stages you practice the facets of openness and curiosity to help you stand in wonder. I think of Carey Smith and his intelligent naiveté as he named himself Chief Big Ass of Big Ass Fans and built his dream based on his ideals.

When you bring more intention to an unconscious process, it can trigger reactions in other people. Some people may want to stop you because your wide-eyed audacity threatens them and their own paradigm of what is rational. Some detractors often think they're acting out of care for you and want you to avoid failure. When Marc and Angel Chernoff wanted to leave their comfortable jobs and devote their full attention to developing a business model based on offering inspiration and coaching for their growing online audience, every member of their financially minded family tried to stop them. They stood in wonder and have since authored a *New York Times* bestseller, and they host an annual conference—Live Better, Think Better—that has allowed them to help tens of thousands of people take agency over their emotions and live happier lives.

When you encounter detractors, you might react with fear. What keeps smart, imaginative people from pursuing their potentially impactful ideas? Lack of time and resources? When I informally polled our community, they told me about their fears. Fear shuts people down—regardless of their profession or station in life—from achieving their potential, especially if they haven't worked out their devotion muscle enough and learned to manage uncertainty. Fear crops up when you start to believe other people's opinions of you more than you believe in your genius and the potential impact of your own ideas. I see fear commonly take these three forms:

FEAR OF LOOKING FOOLISH OR NAIVE. We all seek credibility in our domain, but if we think our ideas may be received as unsophisticated, we feel vulnerable putting ourselves out there and saying, "This is who I am. This is what I'm doing."

FEAR OF CRITICISM, BACKLASH, AND VULNERABILITY. One person in our community wrote, "With anything new, there's so much uncertainty around your idea landing and catching on. You have to be willing to show up, then keep showing up and asking why it isn't working when it doesn't. This is so vulnerable and can feel really lonely. Being in uncertainty and vulnerability for extended amounts of time is taxing."

FEAR OF FAILING, WASTING RESOURCES, AND BEING IRRESPONSIBLE. Many people express a fear of wasting their time and limited resources with no clear return on their investment. One person wrote, "There's a constant pull back to our conditioning that 'risk equals irresponsibility,' and then you just get exhausted justifying yourself to other people for why you're taking the risks you are."

Yet no fulfilled creative life came from choosing a path based solely on what others think. It takes practice that can often extend over years to feel confident in your creations, but it's important to learn this one technique for deflecting detractors from your wondrous path.

Invitation: Give a Miles Davis Shrug to Others' Nay-Saying

Few tunes bring out my creative wonder more deliriously and instantly than Miles Davis's landmark tune "So What." It's the first track of *Kind of Blue*, hands down the bestselling jazz record of all time. Released in 1959, the album of six tracks defied the standard bebop trend of jazz at the time and forever changed the way people thought of jazz, and it changed the way musicians played.

I hear in the two-note refrain on "So What" Davis's nonchalant shrug to the musical establishment. When you hear that chorus of the status quo or the peer peanut gallery start to chime in with "But what if you fail? But what if you lose money? But what about your obligations?" then respond (silently or otherwise) with your own shrug of confident cool: "So what?"

Reflect on these questions and write down your responses in specific language:

Who do I think is going to criticize my ventures? Who do I feel I would be embarrassed in front of? Do these people really care about my fulfillment, or is their criticism more about their projections?

Are these the very people who might ultimately benefit from my pursuing this dream? If not, *who* are the people that I care about who could benefit?

> What's the worst that could happen
> if I shrugged toward the detractors
> with a Miles Davis "So what?"

Write down in specific language how you will shrug off unwanted criticism. This way your self-defined language can help you prepare for inevitable critique. Now imagine what kind of coolheaded confidence could come from a jazzy shrug like that. Maybe find the song and listen to it with your full attention. Several of my clients have found it helpful to write down specific responses to these questions above and then take the extra step to imagine, role-play, and write out how they might respond should someone raise objections.

Here is what I want to say to you: Take the counterintuitive approach and respond to the fear of looking naive by *embracing* your *intelligent* naiveté. Throw out cynicism and convention and connect to the wondrous, devoted feelings that drive you to make the difference that matters.

When you actively foster a sense of open wonder, you connect your devotion to that space of beautiful possibility that expands way beyond the peanut gallery.

DEDICATE A SPACE FOR WONDER

When you stand in wonder, you will experience moments of "Oh my gosh! What am I doing?" Inevitably in the process of advancing a worthwhile endeavor, you will see a gap between your vision of a realized idea and the reality of making it happen. At this stage you learn how tracking wonder helps you embrace rather than flee from uncertainty.

Think of the chapters on bewilderment and hope and how these facets build resilience and fortitude. Here you get into the habit of testing your curiosity and iterating for multiple possible solutions. I think of Tracy Fullerton patiently testing out her dream to turn the nonfiction book *Walden* into a contemplative educational video game. I think of Nick Cave asking his fans for honest conversation during his period of grief.

To ground your mind and stand in wonder, you can devote a physical space—however small or large—to act like a safe, brave, and playful container for your insights. It can be a table, garden, woodshop, corner, garage, converted closet, room, or part of your office. Annie Dillard wrote her Pulitzer Prize–winning first book *Pilgrim at Tinker Creek* in a tiny shed, so you need not envision elaborate work spaces to start making your brave Wonder Lab.

You can experiment with physical cues. There's a growing science to understanding the mystery and beauty of how space can affect us on a sensory level.

Invitation: Create an Open Vibe and Bring the Outdoors Inside

Here's an invitation: see, smell, and touch this physical space in a wholly new and wondrous way. Remember, wonder is often subtle, so even small changes can create lingering effects.

We know that mice, rats, and primates, for instance, grow more neurons in the hippocampus when they are raised not in sterile steel cages but in enriched environments that mimic a natural setting. When we humans get back to our natural setting, similar effects emerge. A joint study by the University of Kansas and the University of Utah showed that people who hiked and camped for three days increased their creativity scores by 50 percent.

But if you can't easily take a forest walk or head off to camp in the middle of the week, you can bring the outdoors into your work space. Gaze for forty seconds at a nature scene—a poster on a wall or a screen saver. More than one study shows that doing so can restore your tired mind, help you focus, and solve creative problems more effectively. It's also important to integrate regular breaks with outdoor activity. Just popping out for a five-minute walk—especially near water—can reenergize you for the next step.

I also have had this abiding obsession about parts of houses where you could steal away, hide, and dream. Nooks and crannies, makeshift forts made of chairs and blankets, small closets transformed into reading nests—that sort of thing. In the architect Christopher Alexander's marvelous book *A Pattern Language*, he describes "child-caves." Children, he notes, "seek out cave-like spaces to get into and under—old crates, under tables, in tents." Kristopher KC Carter—a friend who is a combo of consultant, rocking musician whose podcast airs on Ani DiFranco's network, and jubilant father of three children—routinely transforms a room into an entire cardboard fort. I suspect the fort is as much for him as for his kids.

I think our grown-up young geniuses seek them out, too. You can break up your space—no matter how small or vast—into a zone or two. For instance, when I redesigned my study after the fire, I wanted it to feel like a modest creative laboratory with various stations for different activities.

My get-it-done zone includes a standing desk on wheels, a laptop on a raised platform, a second monitor and printer on a nearby table, a wireless keypad, and a timer. A pilot study by Ranjana K. Mehta of Texas A&M University concluded that stand-up desks can boost your executive functioning—that part of your cognition that helps you focus, analyze, retrieve relevant memories, and advance complex endeavors. Stand-up desks don't have to be fancy. Some clients have engineered standing desks by stacking milk cartons atop tables. I use mine to move projects forward in a highly focused manner, particularly my client video strategy sessions.

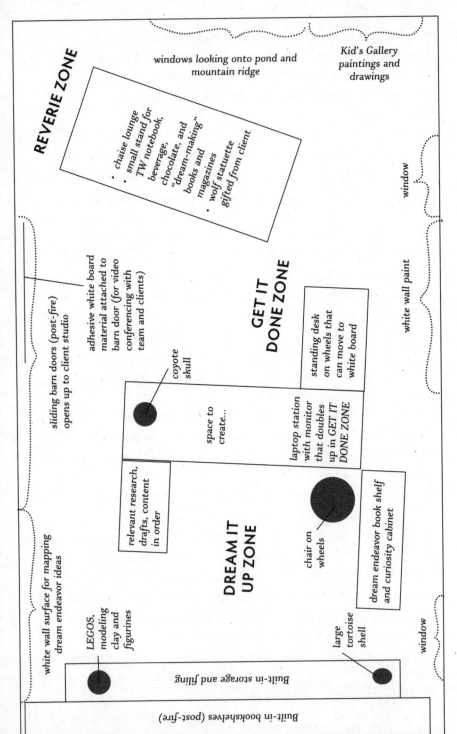

REVERIE ZONE

windows looking onto pond and mountain ridge

Kid's Gallery paintings and drawings

- chaise lounge
- small stand for TW notebook, beverage, chocolate, and "dream-making" books and magazines
- wolf statuette gifted from client

sliding barn doors (post-fire) opens up to client studio

adhesive white board material attached to barn door (for video conferencing with team and clients)

GET IT DONE ZONE

coyote skull

space to create...

standing desk on wheels that can move to white board

relevant research, drafts, content in order

laptop station with monitor that doubles up in GET IT DONE ZONE

DREAM IT UP ZONE

chair on wheels

dream endeavor book shelf and curiosity cabinet

white wall surface for mapping dream endeavor ideas

LEGOS, modeling clay and figurines

large tortoise shell

Built-in storage and filing

Built-in bookshelves (post-fire)

window

white wall paint

window

A sketch of the author's ever-shifting Wonder Lab zones.

Invitation: Choose One Zone

If you could make one small adjustment to your physical space and refine one zone, which one would it be? If you answer yes to more of these statements in one zone versus another, choose that zone to create or improve.

Get-It-Done Zone

I value action but often get distracted from my dream endeavor.

I often waste time remembering where I put supplies necessary to execute my endeavor.

I want to feel more energized, focused, and confident as I advance my endeavor, one step at a time.

Dream-It-Up Zone

I value the idea conception and formation and want a space to spread out resources, notes, and ideas.

I want space devoted to conceiving, forming, and pulling together ideas.

I want to feel more playful and open-minded in exploring my ideas in action.

Reverie Zone

I value deliberate daydreaming.

Yet when fatigued, I often "zone out" with digital distractions instead of "zone in" with deliberate daydreaming.

I want a space that will encourage me to relax in a creative way.

Start small. Take one step that will make a difference in how your mind responds to the new zone.

GIFT WONDER

The art that matters to us—which moves the heart, or revives the soul, or delights the senses, or offers courage for living, however we choose to describe the experience— that work is received by us as a gift is received.

LEWIS HYDE

author of *The Gift*

Something in us aches at times to elevate others. That urge is as innate, natural, and biological as is a child's urge to make something out of paper and marker and give it to someone special. And the thing is, you can create such artful memorable moments. That power to alter situations and enhance minds for the better is in its most elevated form when we gift wonder to others.

At a certain stage, you will want to share the fruits of your endeavor and embrace the exchange of wonder. This stage is about bringing your endeavor—and yourself—into the public arena on your own terms, especially with the facets of connection and admiration. Doing so doesn't have to be flashy and self-centered. Instead, you instill admiration in others by developing your own public style and designing delightful experiences for other people.

Remember that experiencing wonder disrupts our default biased ways of plodding through our days, of assuming that our subjective sense of reality is true for all, of keeping our heads down and noses to the grindstone. For a moment that can ripple for a lifetime, wonder removes the film from our eyes and clears the fog from our brains. The world-renowned installation artist Julianne Swartz told me, "I'm definitely looking to provoke an experience of unfamiliarity or surprise or disorientation. I think all of those are productive openings for wonder." We all have the power to offer memorable, surprising experiences and insight to those people whom we love, care about, and serve.

I discovered a powerful story of gifting wonder from Hollye Dexter, a mom to three and creative writer in Los Angeles. As the isolation of stay-at-home orders began in the spring of 2020, Hollye watched her fourteen-year-old son grow more and more depressed. Busy with their own work and unable to bring him out of his shell, Hollye and her husband, Troy, wondered what they could do to connect with their son and lift his spirits. They were supposed to have spent the spring break in New York City, seeing Broadway shows and indulging in the delights of the big city. But just because they were stuck at home didn't mean they had to completely miss out on New York.

Hollye and Troy decided to make a destination dinner for their son. "Don't come out of your room until dinner," they told him, and then set about transforming their living space into a version of Times Square. They dug through their basement for supplies they could upcycle into skyscrapers and landmarks. They made a playlist of New York tunes. They ordered Domino's Pizza but then changed the box with the label of a famous Manhattan pizzeria. When their son emerged from his room, his sullen face lit up. He couldn't believe what his parents had done. Hollye said her son's true personality emerged, and they enjoyed feeling as if they were transported to their destination for the whole evening. They sang, played games, and delighted in the wonder of an evening away. At the end of the night, her son said, "Okay, where are we going tomorrow night?"

That question launched the family on a journey to over forty destination dinners, and they're still going. For each weekend festivity, Hollye and Troy take whole days to prepare props, special menus, and activities based on locations such as Japan, India, Africa, even outer space. Their rule is that they have to create everything from stuff they have lying around home. "I spent hours crafting a didgeridoo for our Australia night," Hollye said, "and I knew it would only be used for this one occasion, but it gave me so much joy to throw myself into this project, it was like therapy for me. I don't know how we would have gotten through the quarantine without our destination dinners."

This remarkable inspiration, sprung from wanting to help her son recapture his sense of joy and wonder, motivated the family to get through a hard time. Gifting wonder could have been what saved their son from sliding down the slippery slope of depression. No matter how simple or elaborate your efforts are, if you can tap into what sparks wonder for others, you can bring more light and life into the world. Every creator knows that this is the most supreme satisfaction. Connecting with others in wonder is, I believe, the most powerful gesture of love.

Invitation: Gift Wonder

How can you apply your talents to the challenge of gifting wonder? Consider who's going to benefit from your endeavor or who could benefit just from your sharing it. Based on my research and experience in working with people in this arena, I've discovered six core types of experiences that are especially memorable and meaningful to people. Fortunately, these six types of moments form a memorable acronym: **CREATE**.

Curiosity experiences spark inquisitiveness, surprise, and delightful uncertainty. Cory, a manager of a startup in

Austin, Texas, returned from one of my workshops ready to awaken his team's creative geniuses. He told me he had noticed how at team meetings, everyone arrived in default mode. Dim inner lights. Arms folded. As soon as they walked in, they were ready to leave. So Cory stepped back and wondered what simple intervention he could include to stoke his team's curiosity from the onset. He decided that each week he'd begin by switching up the meeting locale. One week a meeting might be in a closed-off room. The next week, in the eating area. The next week, in the outdoor patio. That simple shift did two things: it prompted Cory to mix up the meeting tone and focus each week; and the different locales simply kept everyone a little "off balance," not knowing what to expect.

How could you pique someone's curiosity?

How could you give them hints or partial information or raise a fun question before the experience, event, or "revelation"? People love fun suspense. Withhold information to entice people to want to learn or be more creative.

Raise relevant yet provocative questions.

Disrupt routine expectations.

Recognition experiences are moments that offer opportunities for insight, renewal, and discovery in which people see themselves, other people, a concept, or a situation anew.

How could you celebrate someone's important milestone in a memorable way?

How could you bring wonder to conventional celebrations such as birthdays, retirements, or award ceremonies?

How could you facilitate surprising admiration between people or someone's self-admiration and self-recognition for their excellence?

Emotional peak experiences allow people to feel deeply and elevated in surprising ways.

Consider how to arouse novel sensory stimulation—music, art, natural beauty—to heighten nonverbal responses.

Encourage the sharing of personal stories.

If you host large events or conferences, remember that not everyone is a raging extrovert. Create hubs for emotional connection. Your event will be that much more meaningful and memorable.

Check out Dr. Arthur Aron's "36 Questions to Fall in Love." We've adapted these questions at different stages in our events to help people bond near instantly.

Afterglow experiences deepen meaningful memory after the experience has passed. At the close of our events, we've done things such as dash to a building roof in SoHo, New York City, to huddle in the rain and howl.

Create a simple ceremony or ritual to make an experience's wonder linger.

Make a simple memento of a wondrous moment you had with someone else and send it to them.

After a meaningful experience with other people, ask each person or participant to pause and reflect on one personal sensory highlight from the experience.

Transcendent experiences of full immersion and flow let us be at our genius best and allow us to move beyond our perceived limitations. Our live events often have Dolphin Tank sessions (friendlier, smarter, and more creative than "Shark Tanks") that require participants to "stand and pitch" an idea to the group. Given that public speaking mortifies most people, you can see how a four-minute exercise can help people transcend their self-limitations. One person who's attended many such events confided that she used to abhor Dolphin Tanks. Now, with a newfound courage, she relishes them.

How could you help someone face a fear and develop a strength?

How can you encourage people to reach beyond comfort zones and into brave zones?

Expansion experiences help us feel bonded and connected to something, someone, or some group beyond our self and our self-limitations. They can fulfill the core human need to belong and feel connected to a greater purpose.

Create experiments that require people to collaborate and create something together.

Provide moments for people to show that they understand and care about one another.

Facilitate moments for people to realize the mission, values, ideals, and dreams they hold in common.

You really don't know how your gift of wonder will ripple in ways you may never see. When eleven-year-old Amy Sherald visited a museum in Georgia, she didn't expect to be given a gift that would last a lifetime, but that is how she describes it. The artist told a *New York Times* reporter that at that museum she saw the Black painter Bo Bartlett's self-portrait *Object Permanence*. For the first time, she says she "experienced the power of seeing a painting of a person who looked like me. I essentially built my career around that moment and created an inflection point for someone else." In the same interview, she notes how she wants to keep open to the diversity of "the Black experience."

"I want to explore," she says, "the wonder of what it is to be a Black American. And the complexity of that identity. I want the everydayness of the people to psychologically stay with you and change how you interact with others." Sherald says she wants her work to be "a gift" to the Black public because of the moment that seeing Bartlett's painting gifted her.

Sherald's wish came true. She was tapped by Michelle Obama to paint the first lady's portrait. In 2018, a two-year-old Black girl, Parker Curry, saw the portrait at the National Portrait Gallery. She stood spellbound, her mouth agape. When her mother tried to turn her daughter around for a picture, the girl refused to lose her gaze. According to one witness, everyone else in the room grew silent as they witnessed the moment. "It's hard to describe in words," the witness told a reporter. "She had such wonder on her face and her entire body just stopped as she looked at her, and she had this wonder that was silent and yet seemed to be saying something very big at the same time."

That's one way wonder ripples.

When we stand in wonder we can be agents of wonder's ripples not only for ourselves but also for one another, if not for the greater good. I turn to the Lakota people's language to get a fresh perspective. One meaning of the Lakota word *itonpa* is "to be astonished, to wonder, to praise." We might extend genuine *itonpa* toward sudden snowfall or the insight a child's comment gives us. Yet itonpa also means "to care for, to tend to."

What we are in wonder with, we are more prone to care for. For our species there is much that we could care for and so create wiser, more wondrous ways to be on this planet together. Let's stand for that.

FIVE WISHES OF WONDER FOR THIS ONE LIFE

IN TRUE DIT SPIRIT, I am humbled by my limitations. You and the people that you know, live with, and work with possess geniuses, talents, and skills that can be applied to reclaiming our birthright to wonder. We must do this as we pursue uncharted possibilities—without wrecking our species or planet in the process.

These are my five wishes for how we might spread wonder for the greater good. Maybe one of them calls to you.

WISH 1: BRING WONDER HOME

The father who has denied his wonder and has ignored *his* young genius might bristle at the sight of a child embracing their own genius. Yet there are bountiful opportunities for us to foster relationships based on wonder with our loved ones. Once we remember and reclaim our own young genius, we could be more likely to generously welcome our partners, parents, and children to follow their own. I think of Brandy Donovan, who put up a Wonder Wall for her family to express what they wonder about each day. I think of Barb Buckner Suárez, whose family of six often rotates with each person raising a point of reflective conversation at dinnertime. I think of what the social workers and family organizations who provide services and education to parents could do. Wonder is not the province of privilege. Wonder is the birthright of every child. Why not get better practiced at seeing again the beauty of the people we grow most familiar with?

WISH 2: RETURN WONDER AS THE MOTOR OF LEARNING

In this age of rampant change, wonder is the reset button that counters panic and fuels innovative curiosity. That fact has consequences for how we could design and allow for human learning in the twenty-first century—for geniuses of all ages. According to Todd Rose and Ogi Ogas—cofounders of the Dark Horse Project out of Harvard Graduate School of Education—we are passing beyond the age of standardization (think, *test, test, test* and *compare and compete*) to the age of customization (think, *follow your quirky curiosities*). I think of Cristian Fracassi, who could quickly iterate and create a ventilator part and save lives in Italy. I think of the filmmaker George Lucas's foundation, Edutopia, that aims to distribute new best practices in what often looks like wonder-centric education. I think of the many educators and advocates for renewed education who yearn to design human learning in ways that honor the truth of what Socrates told Theaetetus, a too-certain young mathematician over a millennia ago: wonder is the beginning of wisdom.

To teachers, deans, managers, and anyone involved in learning, I invite you to entertain these and other questions: What if more people involved in educating others supported the art of questioning just as much as having the right answers? How could you keep fostering a healthy uncertainty and curiosity in people so they continued to love learning itself?

WISH 3: BRING WONDER TO WORK

We industrious human beings spend vast hours a week working, yet our prevailing culture still diminishes workers. If the poet Kahlil Gibran could be right in saying that "work is love made manifest," then we have a lot of work to do to bring a sense of wonder to the heart of our work and, for leaders, to the heart of our workplaces. Recognizing the genius in one another, fostering connection and admiration among team members, designing workplaces conducive to wondering, and having supportive conditions to take wonder breaks are only small steps, but they are a start.

To managers, leaders, and business owners of many varieties, how could you invite more wonder into your workplace? To start-up founders, funders, and legislators, how could you be in wonder in reimagining work and its institutions in ways that truly uplift the genius in everyone?

WISH 4: BRING WONDER
TO THE MIND

So many talented psychologists, mindfulness teachers, and other spelunkers of the human psyche are on the trail of wonder. Yes, wonder's subtle nature and primal status means it often evades conventional human measurements. But maybe that very conundrum of this first-of-all emotions points us back to honoring the mysteries of our nature. The human mind is rife with biases. What would happen if we imbued more of our examinations of human bias with a greater appreciation for surprising moments when those biases dissolve? We can be quick to do battle with our own thinking minds and to pathologize the human mind in general. Yet the mind is what it is—complex, mysterious, and the very vehicle through which we can apprehend the beauty of the world and our own beautiful nature.

To psychologists, neuroscientists, mindfulness teachers, and organizational consultants, how might we ask different questions that lead to a deeper understanding of our capacity for and benefits of experiencing wonder?

WISH 5: APPRECIATE THE WONDER
OF OUR HOME PLANET

If wisdom begins in wonder, I'm convinced that wonder begins in nature. I think of that hooting chimp gawking at the waterfall for no reason other than he must. I think of Rachel Carson who, upon seeing for the first time the wide-open ocean horizon, shifted her major from writing to marine biology, and how that moment of her wonder forever altered the course of modern humans' understanding of our relationship to the earth. Convinced that a healthy change in how we related to earth began in childhood, she reached out directly to mothers in 1956 by publishing an essay titled "Help Your Child to Wonder" in *Woman's Home Companion*. The gist: children remind us that we are not apart from nature but a part of nature.

I think of the bountiful individuals such as the wildlife biologist and tortoise tracker Imogen Daly and members of organizations who stand up for the rights of endangered species and marginalized people adversely harmed by our degradation of natural resources. I also try to imagine what would happen if those organizations' leaders evoked more genuine wonder toward the natural world we inhabit and are part and parcel of.

Lovers of the earth, how can you share your wondrous experiences in nature more widely and impact our ability to care for our common home?

— —

There is an urge in us as natural as the process of autumn's cold nights conspiring with maple leaves in October to set valleys ablaze with shades of poppies and burgundies, of golds and lemons, of peaches and apricots. You could be driving through such a valley, car windows cracked so the cool air ruffles your hair and calms your mind, and as the fiery paintings pass by on either side, you might wonder aloud, "My god! How can I contribute something like *that*?" You can't match nature's sublime beauty, of course, but you can recognize that the creative force within nature also infuses your genius to give, spread, and perpetuate wonder. As Melvin Konner reminded us early in this book, it's our choice.

We are given this one life with its infinite potential, and each day and each week has a finite number of hours. We're here to make the most of it, every day. We can wonder this world into even more beauty for all of us.

So much is possible.

— —

Thanks for running with me.

ACKNOWLEDGMENTS

"A dream you dream alone is only a dream.
A dream you dream together is reality."

YOKO ONO

WHAT IF THE BYLINE of every book more accurately reflected all of the people who invisibly brought forward and shaped that book? No cover could hold it.

This dream endeavor would never have been realized without this extraordinary support pack.

No idea exists in isolation. It is only from the ongoing conversation and exploration of wonder for the past few thousand years that this book can offer its verse to the ongoing conversation. I am indebted to numerous psychologists, philosophers, anthropologists, archaeologists, animal trackers, theologians, neurologists, biologists, physicists, environmentalists, entomologists, entrepreneurs, leaders, poets, artists, and teachers whose work in one way or another shaped this book.

Jaime Schwalb of Sounds True saw the promise of this book early on (I miss our New York City lunches) and has been a wise, savvy champion of the book through every stage. Thank you for helping me dream bigger, Jaime. Jessica Carew Kraft applied her editorial deftness and tracking wisdom to our seeing anew this book's form, focus, and so much more. Emily Wichland of Sounds True provided elegant copyediting—an oft unheralded art that merits admiration—under the careful guidance of production editor Laurel Szmyd. Designers Jennifer Miles and Linsey Dodaro of Sounds True "nailed it" with how design contributes to a reader's delightfully surprising experience. A special call-out to Holly Moxley—thank you for trusting me long ago to grow our Tracking Wonder Team and then to return to translate my rough sketches into this book's elegant facet icons. And Tami Simon, thank you for staying true to your original vision with Sounds True of how business as unusual can be done with integrity, decade after decade.

As much as this lone wolf often runs in solitude, I am grateful to have dear friends and colleagues who have provided counsel and supportive shoulders along the way. Charlie Gilkey, thank you, my wise younger brother-by-choice, for seeing all those years ago the promise in this Tracking Wonder endeavor, for helping the wonder medicine to reach more people, and for knowing the kind of collaboration this book needed. Jayme Johnson and the crew at Worthy Marketing Group offered exceptional marketing and communication support. Noah Levy contributed his zest for ideas and pitching. Pam Slim offered ongoing counsel in assembling the right support pack to realize this book's potential and for the life-after-book-launch wisdom. Jonathan Fields, thank you for seeing me in beautiful ways I cannot fully see myself and for readily offering your friendship on this journey. Eric Klein, thank you for peeking at early ideas for this book's proposal and offering sage perspective. Blair Glaser, our "power hour" talks consistently helped me get grounded in otherwise bewildering times.

The Tracking Wonder Team, past and present, first taught me the lessons of Do It Together. Thank you to Jenny Sudo, Laine Ann Baldocchi, Britt Bravo, Hillary Lyons, Dom John, Susan Preston, the team at Rocket Publicidad, and Laureen Clinton as well as to Erin Haworth, Tanya Robie, Heidi Johnson, Julia Gilmor, and Michele Mangen.

This book would never have been realized without all of the Airbnb hosts in the Catskill Mountains who over the years provided me inspiring, quiet space for my deep dive retreats.

I am deeply grateful to all of the geniuses of creativity who have contributed their stories to this book.

And to the Tracking Wonder Community at large, I am especially grateful for all you have taught me about the wisdom of wonder in the world. You made this dream real.

Mom, thank you for letting that tow-headed boy's young genius lead him where he needed to go for nourishment—Fort Worth's woods, art museums, libraries, and Japanese Garden. You saw me the way I needed to be seen.

To my daughters, Dahlia and Alethea, you daily teach me more about what tracking wonder looks like. Thank you for claiming your young geniuses every single day—and for letting mine come out to play and grow with yours.

Thank you to Hillary, my wife and partner. On a walk in the woods many moons ago, as I talked out this nascent endeavor about wonder, she said, "Oh, you're tracking wonder." She never once stopped seeing this dream's value, reshaped at least two chapters, and provided lots of invisible deep dive support. Thank you for letting me live the wisdom of standing in love.

Do it together does beat do it yourself.

BIBLIOGRAPHY

Introduction

William Blake, *The Marriage of Heaven and Hell* (Boston: John W. Luce, 1906), gutenberg.org/files/45315/45315-h/45315-h.htm.

Martha Nussbaum, *Upheavals of Thought: The Intelligence of Emotions*, 8th ed. (Cambridge: Cambridge University Press, 2008), chaps. 4 and 6.

René Descartes, *The Passions of the Soul*, trans. and ann. Stephen Vess (Indianapolis: Hackett, 1989), 52.

Plato, *Theaetetus*, trans. Benjamin Jowett (New York: Charles Scribner's Sons, 1871), sacred-texts.com/cla/plato/theaetet.htm.

Chapter 1   Flames

Jaideva Singh, *Siva Sutras: The Yoga of Supreme Identity* (Delhi: Motilal Banarsidass Publishers, 2003), 52.

Chapter 2   Biases Against Wonder

Melvin Konner, *The Tangled Wing: Biological Constraints on the Human Spirit* (New York: Henry Holt, 2002), 485–87.

René Descartes, *The Passions of the Soul*, trans. and ann. Stephen Vess (Indianapolis: Hackett, 1989), 52.

"The Work Martyr's Cautionary Tale: How the Millennial Experience Will Define America's Vacation Culture," U.S. Travel Association, August 18, 2016, ustravel.org/research/work-martyr's-cautionary-tale-how-millennial-experience-will-define-america's-vacation.

Derek Thompson, "The Religion of Workism Is Making Americans Miserable," *The Atlantic*, February 24, 2019, theatlantic.com/ideas/archive/2019/02/religion-workism-making-americans-miserable/583441/.

Joseph Wright, "wonderment, 2, 3," in *The English Dialect Dictionary* (Oxford: Oxford University Press, 1905), 534.

Chapter 3   The Six Facets of Wonder

Mark Elbroch, in discussion with the author, October 2006.

Kelly Bulkeley, *The Wondering Brain: Thinking about Religion with and Beyond Cognitive Neuroscience* (New York: Routledge, 2005), 4.

Jonathan Haidt, phone interview, April 2012.

Your Young Genius

Darya L. Zabelina and Michael D. Robinson, "Child's Play: Facilitating the Originality of Creative Output by a Priming Manipulation," *Psychology of Aesthetics, Creativity, and the Arts* 4, no. 1 (2010): 57–65.

Denise Markonish and Julianne Swartz, "What If We Could Explode Every Day?" October 30, 2018, in *Tracking Wonder*, podcast, audio, 1:06:31, trackingwonder.com/podcast/if-we-could-explode-every-day.

Plato, *The Republic*, trans. Allan Bloom (New York: Basic Books, 2016).

James Hillman, *The Soul's Code: In Search of Character and Calling* (New York: Grand Central Publishing, 1996).

Chip Heath and Chris Flink, "Experience Design to Build Wonder at Work," October 16, 2018, in *Tracking Wonder*, podcast, audio, 01:12:12, trackingwonder.com/podcast/experience-design-build -wonder-at-work.

Arianna Huffington, *The Gods of Greece* (New York: Atlantic Monthly Press, 1993), 129.

Evelyn Asher, email correspondence, September 2020.

Heath and Flink, "Experience Design to Build Wonder at Work."

Charles Baudelaire, "The Painter of Modern Life," *The Painter of Modern Life and Other Essays*, trans. Jonathan Mayne (New York: Phaidon Press, 2001), 6.

Henri Matisse, "Art: Captain Pablo's Voyages," *Time*, June 26, 1950, content.time.com/time/subscriber/article/0,33009,857821-5,00.html.

Dorie Clark and Jonathan Fields, "Finessing a Healthy Competition," May 22, 2018, in *Tracking Wonder*, podcast, audio, 59:26, trackingwonder.com/podcast/competition-community-dorie-clark -jonathan-fields.

Chapter 4   Openness, the Wide-Sky Facet

Henry D. Thoreau, *The Illustrated "Walden" with Photographs from the Gleason Collection* (Princeton, NJ: Princeton University Press, 1973), 324.

Mihaly Csikszentmihalyi, *Creativity: Flow and the Psychology of Discovery and Invention* (New York: Harper Perennial, 1996), 59–60.

Scott Barry Kaufman et al. "Openness to Experience and Intellect Differentially Predict Creative Achievement in the Arts and Sciences," *Journal of Personality* 84, no. 2 (2016): 248–58, doi.org/10 .1111/jopy.12156.

Sen Xu, Xueting Jiang, and Ian J. Walsh, "The Influence of Openness to Experience on Perceived Employee Creativity: The Moderating Roles of Individual Trust," *Journal of Creative Behavior* 52, no. 2 (June 2018): 142–55.

Carey Smith, interview with Mike O'Toole, "Big Ass Fans," October 12, 2012, in *The Unconventionals*, podcast, audio, 00:29, podcasts.apple .com/us/podcast/big-ass-fans/id571972797?i=1000169863677.

Ray Dalio, *Principles* (New York: Simon & Schuster, 2017), ix.

Ming Hsu, Meghana Bhatt, Ralph Adolphs, Daniel Tranel, and Colin F. Camerer, "Neural Systems Responding to Degrees of Uncertainty in Human Decision-Making," *Science*, 310, no. 5754 (December 9, 2005): 1680–83, doi.org/10.1126/science.1115327.

Scott Barry Kaufman and Carolyn Gregoire, *Wired to Create: Unraveling the Mysteries of the Creative Mind* (New York: Perigree, 2015), 83.

Charles Baxter, "Stillness," *Burning Down the House: Essays on Fiction*, exp. ed. (Minneapolis: Graywolf Press, 2008), 195.

Dacher Keltner, in interview with author, November 2011.

Kareem J. Johnson, Christian E. Waugh, and Barbara L. Fredrickson, "Smile to See the Forest: Facially Expressed Positive Emotions Broaden Cognition," *Cognition and Emotion* 24, no. 2 (2010): 299–321, doi.org/10.1080/02699930903384667.

Joe Hinds and Paul Sparks, "The Affective Quality of Human-Natural Environment Relationships," *Evolutionary Psychology* 9, vol. 3 (2011): 451–69, doi.org/10.1177/147470491100900314.

Nancy C. Andreasen, *The Creative Brain: The Science of Genius* (New York: Plume, 2005), 32.

Jack Cowart and Juan Hamilton, "#14 To Anita Pollitzer," *Georgia O'Keeffe: Art and Letters*, ed. Sarah Greenbough (New York: Little, Brown, 1987), 157.

Chapter 5 Curiosity, the Rebel Facet

Cristian Fracassi, email interview with author, May 30, 2020.

Todd B. Kashdan and Michael F. Steger, "Curiosity and Pathways to Well-Being and Meaning in Life: Traits, States, and Everyday Behaviors," *Motivation and Emotion* 31 (2007): 159–73, doi.org/10 .1007/s11031-007-9068-7.

Todd B. Kashdan, *Curious: Discover the Missing Ingredient to a Fulfilling Life* (New York: William Morrow, 2009).

Mihaly Csikszentmihalyi, *Creativity: Flow and the Psychology of Discovery and Invention* (New York: Harper Perennial, 1996), 87.

Catherine L'Ecuyer, "The Wonder Approach to Learning," *Frontiers in Human Neuroscience* 8 (October 6, 2014), doi.org/10.3389/fnhum.2014.00764.

Matthias J. Gruber, Bernard D. Gelman, and Charan Ranganath, "States of Curiosity Modulate Hippocampus-Dependent Learning via the Dopaminergic Circuit," *Neuron* 84, no. 2 (2014): 486–96, doi.org/10.1016/j.neuron.2014.08.060.

Paul A. O'Keefe, Carol S. Dweck, and Gregory M. Walton, "Implicit Theories of Interest: Finding Your Passion or Developing It?" *Psychological Science* 29, no. 10 (2018): 1653–64, doi.org/10.1177/0956797618780643.

Colin G. DeYoung, "The Neuromodulator of Exploration: A Unifying Theory of the Role of Dopamine in Personality," *Frontiers in Human Neuroscience* 7 (2013): 762.

Srini Pillay and Alex Soojung-Kim Pang, "The Power of Deliberate Unfocus, Rest, & Daydreaming," November 6, 2018, in *Tracking Wonder*, podcast, audio, 01:04:02, trackingwonder.com/podcast/episode-004.

Oliver Sacks, *Everything in Its Place: First Loves and Last Tales* (New York: Knopf, 2019).

Barb Buckner Suárez, email conversation, November 10, 2020.

Barb Buckner Suárez, "About," BB Suárez, bbsuarez.com/about/.

Alan Lightman, interview with Harry Stimpson, "Questions with Answers and Questions Without: A Profile of Alan Lightman," *Poets & Writers*, November/December 2007.

Katie Hafner, "Scientist at Work: Dr. Donald A. Redelmeier; Think the Answer's Clear? Look Again," *New York Times*, August 30, 2010, nytimes.com/2010/08/31/science/31profile.html.

Donald A. Redelmeier, "The Cognitive Psychology of Missed Diagnoses," *Annals of Internal Medicine* 142 (2005): 115–20, doi.org/10.7326/0003-4819-142-2-200501180-00010.

Maja Djikic, Keith Oatley, and Mihnea C. Moldoveanu, "Opening the Closed Mind: The Effect of Exposure to Literature on the Need for Closure," *Creativity Research Journal* 25, no. 2 (2013): 149–54, doi.org/10.1080/10400419.2013.783735.

Peter Sims, *Little Bets: How Breakthrough Ideas Emerge from Small Discoveries* (New York: Simon and Schuster, 2013).

Stephen Greenblatt, *Marvelous Possessions: The Wonder of the New World* (Chicago: University of Chicago Press, 1992).

Mark Osborne and Tracy Fullerton, "Designing for Stillness & Genius in Film, Video Games," November 6, 2018, in *Tracking Wonder*,

podcast, audio, 01:11:27, trackingwonder.com/podcast/designing-for
-stillness-genius-in-film-video-games.

Chapter 6   Bewilderment, the Deep Woods Facet

Tracey Fullerton and Mark Osborne, "Designing for Stillness & Genius in Film, Video Games," November 6, 2018, in *Tracking Wonder*, podcast, audio, 01:11:27, trackingwonder.com/podcast/designing-for -stillness-genius-in-film-video-games.

Kelly Bulkeley, *The Wondering Brain: Thinking about Religion with and Beyond Cognitive Neuroscience* (New York: Routledge, 2005), 4.

Aimee E. Stahl and Lisa Feigenson, "Observing the Unexpected Enhances Infants' Learning and Exploration," *Science* 348, no. 6230 (2015): 91–94, doi.10.1126/science.aaa3799.

Martin P. Paulus, "The Breathing Conundrum—Interoceptive Sensitivity and Anxiety," *Depression and Anxiety* 20, no. 4 (April 2013): 315–20, doi.10.1002/da.22076.

Kirsty L. Spalding et al., "Dynamics of Hippocampal Neurogenesis in Adult Humans," *Cell* 153, no. 6 (2013): 1219–27, doi.org/10.1016/j.cell .2013.05.002.

Kelly McGonigal, *The Upside of Stress: Why Stress Is Good for You, and How to Get Good at It* (New York: Avery, 2016), 51.

Chapter 7   Hope, the Rainbow Facet

Nikki van Schyndel, *Becoming Wild: Living the Primitive Life on a West Coast Island* (Halfmoon Bay, BC: Caitlin Press, 2014), 62–68.

Kevin Rand and Jennifer Cheavens, "Hope Theory," in *The Oxford Handbook of Positive Psychology*, 2nd ed., ed. C. R. Snyder and Shane J. Lopez (New York: Oxford University Press, 2009; online, 2012). Text references the online edition, doi.org/10.1093/oxfordhb /9780195187243.013.0030.

C. R. Snyder, Hal Shorey, Jennifer Cheavens, Kim Pulvers, Virgil H. Adams III, and Cynthia Wiklund, "Hope and Academic Success in College," *Journal of Educational Psychology* 94, no. 4 (2002): 820–26.

Dr. Shane Lopez, "The Science of Hope: An Interview with Shane Lopez," Taking Charge of Your Health & Well Being, University of Minnesota, accessed November 20, 2020, takingcharge.csh.umn.edu /science-hope-interview-shane-lopez.

Shane J. Lopez, *Making Hope Happen: Create the Future You Want for Yourself and Others* (New York: Atria Books, 2013), 70–73.

Benedictus de Spinoza. *The Chief Works of Benedict de Spinoza*, trans. R. H. M. Elwes (London: George Bell and Sons, 1887), 176.

Thomas A. Langens, "Daydreaming Mediates between Goal Commitment and Goal Attainment in Individuals High in Achievement Motivation," *Imagination, Cognition and Personality* 22, no. 2 (December 2003): 103–15, doi.10.2190/TL8L-MXKE-68E6-UAVB.

Jerome L. Singer, *The Inner World of Daydreaming* (New York: Harper & Row, 1975).

Barbara L. Fredrickson, Michele M. Tugade, Christian E. Waugh, and Gregory R. Larkin, "What Good Are Positive Emotions in Crises? A Prospective Study of Resilience and Emotions Following the Terrorist Attacks on the United States on September 11th, 2001," *Journal of Personality and Psychology* 84, no. 2 (2003): 265–376, doi.10.1037/0022-3514.84.2.365.

Elisabeth Tova Bailey, *The Sound of a Wild Snail Eating* (Chapel Hill, NC: Algonquin Books of Chapel Hill, 2010).

Jessamy Calkin, "Let There Be Light," *The Telegraph*, March 17, 2001, telegraph.co.uk/culture/4722219/Let-there-be-light.html.

"Nick Cave's Son Arthur Dies in Brighton Cliff Fall," *BBC News*, July 15, 2015, bbc.com/news/uk-england-sussex-33533530.

One More Time with Feeling, directed by Andrew Dominik (London: Iconoclast, JW Films, Pulse Films, 2016).

Nick Cave, *The Red Hand Files*, no. 1, September 2018, theredhandfiles .com/writing-challenge-skeleton-tree/.

Martha C. Nussbaum, *Upheavals of Thought: The Intelligence of Emotions*, 8th ed. (Cambridge: Cambridge University Press, 2008), 54.

Czeslaw Milosz, "A Mirrored Gallery," *The Collected Poems: 1931–1987*, trans. Renata Gorczymski (New York: Ecco Press, 1988), 376.

Chapter 8 Connection, the Flock Facet

Vivek Murthy, "Work and the Loneliness Epidemic: Reducing Isolation at Work Is Good for Business," *Harvard Business Review*, September 26, 2017, hbr.org/2017/09/work-and-the-loneliness-epidemic.

David Brooks, "One Neighborhood at a Time," *New York Times*, May 17, 2016, nytimes.com/2016/05/17/opinion/one-neighborhood-at-a -time.html.

Sara H. Konrath, Edward H. O'Brien, and Courtney Hsing, "Changes in Dispositional Empathy in American College Students Over Time: A Meta-Analysis," *Personality and Social Psychology Review* 15, no. 2 (2011), doi.org/10.1177/1088868310377395.

Susan Pinker, *The Village Effect: How Face-to-Face Contact Can Make Us Healthier, Happier, and Smarter* (New York: Spiegel & Grau, 2014).

Barbara L. Fredrickson, *Love 2.0: Finding Happiness and Health in Moments of Connection* (New York: Plume, 2013), 42, 86.

Martha C. Nussbaum, *Upheavals of Thought: The Intelligence of Emotions* (Cambridge: Cambridge University Press, 2003), chap. 4.

Vlad Petre Glăveanu, "Creativity and Wonder," *Journal of Creative Behavior* 53, no. 2 (2019): 171.

Chad Danyluck and Elizabeth Page-Gould, "Social and Physiological Context Can Affect the Meaning of Physiological Synchrony," *Scientific Reports* 9, article 8222 (2019), doi.org/10.1038/s41598-019-44667-5.

Timothy D. Wilson, *Strangers to Ourselves: Discovering the Adaptive Unconscious* (Cambridge, MA: Belknap Press of Harvard University Press, 2002).

Questlove, *Creative Quest* (New York: Ecco Press, 2018).

David Bohm and Mark Edwards, *Changing Consciousness: Exploring the Hidden Source of the Social, Political, and Environmental Crises Facing Our World* (New York: HarperCollins, 1991), 185.

Greg J. Stephens, Lauren J. Silbert, and Uri Hasson, "Speaker–Listener Neural Coupling Underlies Successful Communication," *PNAS* 107, no. 32 (2010), doi.org/10.1073/pnas.1008662107.

Kate Murphy, *You're Not Listening: What You're Missing and Why It Matters* (New York: Celadon Books, 2020).

Kate Murphy, interviewed by Jonathan Fields, "The Art and Science of Listening," March 26, 2020, in *Good Life Project*, podcast, audio, 01:08:29, goodlifeproject.com/podcast/kate-murphy/.

Judith E. Glaser, *Conversational Intelligence: How Great Leaders Build Trust and Get Extraordinary Results* (New York: Routledge, 2016).

Unstoppable, directed by Aaron Lieber (San Clemente, CA: Lieber Films, 2018).

Mary Oliver, "The Kingfisher," *At Blackwood Pond* (Newark, NJ: Audible, 2011).

Chapter 9   Admiration, the Mirror Facet

Dylan Jones, *David Bowie: The Oral History* (New York: Three Rivers Press, 2017).

Charles Darwin, *The Expression of the Emotions in Man and Animals*, definitive ed. (New York: Oxford University Press, 1872, 1998), 269.

Simon Critchley, *Bowie* (New York: OR Books, 2014), 55.

Sara B. Algoe and Jonathan Haidt, "Witnessing Excellence in Action: The 'Other-Praising' Emotions of Elevation, Gratitude, and Admiration," *Journal of Positive Psychology* 4, no. 2 (2009): 105–27, doi.org/10.1080/17439760802650519.

Niels van de Ven, Marcel Zeelenberg, and Rik Pieters, "Why Envy Outperforms Admiration," *Personality and Social Psychology Bulletin* 37, no. 6 (2011), doi.org/10.1177/0146167211400421.

Jonathan Haidt and Dacher Keltner, "Appreciation of Beauty and Excellence," in *Character Strengths and Virtues: A Handbook and Classification*, ed. Christopher Peterson and Martin E. P. Seligman (Oxford: Oxford University Press, 2004), 539.

Lucille Clifton, interviewed by Roland Flint, "Lucille Clifton Talks of Her Books of Poems, including *Good Times*," March 21, 2012, YouTube video, 29:16, youtube.com/watch?v=PPr6EOggzm0.

Christopher Lehmann-Haupt, "Books of the Times: Twenty 1969 Books I'm Keeping in My Library," *New York Times*, December 1, 1969, timesmachine.nytimes.com.

Lucille Clifton, "what the mirror said," *How to Carry Water: Selected Poems* (New York: BOA Editions, 1987), 100.

Lucille Clifton in conversation with Sonia Sanchez and Eisa Davis, "Lucille Clifton & Sonia Sanchez: Mirrors & Windows," October 19, 2016, Cave Canem Foundation, YouTube video, 39:44, youtube.com /watch?v=O8aCnU9oArI.

Dean Keith Simonton, "Artistic Creativity and Interpersonal Relationships Across and Within Generations," *Journal of Personality and Social Psychology* 46, no. 6 (1984): 1273–86, doi.org/10.1037 /0022-3514.46.6.1273.

"John Green: 'I'm Tired of Adults Telling Teenagers They Aren't Smart,'" The Guardian, February 27, 2013, theguardian.com /childrens-books-site/2013/feb/27/john-green-adults-teenagers -smart-interview.

Millie Jackson, in discussion, October 27, 2020.

Cameron Anderson, Michael W. Kraus, and Dacher Keltner, "The Local Ladder Effect: Social Status and Subjective Well-Being," (working paper, Institute for Research on Labor and Employment: Working Paper Series, 2011), escholarship.org/uc/item/2x39c3kp.

Chapter 10   Stand in Wonder

Erich Fromm, *The Art of Loving* (New York: Harper Perennial, 1956), 18.

Mahatma Gandhi, *The Message of the Gita*, compiled by R. K. Prabhu (Gujarat, India: Navajivan Trust, 1959), 26.

Imogen Daly, phone interview, December 2, 2020.

Ruth Ann Atchley, David L. Strayer, and Paul Atchley, "Creativity in the Wild: Improving Creative Reasoning through Immersion in Natural Settings," *PLOS One* (December 12, 2012), doi.org/10.1371/journal.pone.0051474.

Kate E. Lee et al., "40-Second Green Roof Views Sustain Attention: The Role of Micro-Breaks in Attention Restoration," *Journal of Environmental Psychology* 42 (June 2015): 182–89, doi.org/10.1016/j.jenvp.2015.04.003.

Audrey Bergouignan et al., "Effect of Frequent Interruptions of Prolonged Sitting on Self-Perceived Levels of Energy, Mood, Food Cravings and Cognitive Function," *International Journal of Behavioral Nutrition and Physical Activity* 13, no. 113 (2016), doi.org/10.1186/s12966-016-0437-z.

Cristina Vert et al., "Physical and Mental Health Effects of Repeated Short Walks in a Blue Space Environment: A Randomised Crossover Study," *Environmental Research* 188, no. 109812 (September 2020), doi.org/10.1016/j.envres.2020.109812.

Christopher Alexander, *A Pattern Language: Towns, Buildings, Construction* (New York: Oxford University Press, 1977), 928.

Ranjana K. Mehta, Ashley E. Shortz, and Mark E. Benden, "Standing Up for Learning: A Pilot Investigation on the Neurocognitive Benefits of Stand-Biased School Desks," *International Journal of Environmental Research and Public Health* 13, no. 1 (2016), doi.org/10.3390/ijerph13010059.

Denise Markonish and Julianne Swartz, "What If We Could Explode Every Day?" October 30, 2018, in *Tracking Wonder*, podcast, audio, 1:06:31, trackingwonder.com/podcast/if-we-could-explode-every-day.

Hollye Dexter, phone interview, December 1, 2020.

Arthur Aron et al., "The Experimental Generation of Interpersonal Closeness: A Procedure and Some Preliminary Findings," *Personality and Social Psychology Bulletin* 23, no. 4 (1997): 363–77.

Amy Sherald, in conversation with artists Simone Leigh and Lorna Simpson and journalist Jenna Wortham, "I Want to Explore the Wonder of What It Is to Be a Black American," *New York Times Magazine: The Culture Issue*, October 8, 2019.

David Mack, "This Photo of a Little Girl Staring at Michelle Obama's Portrait Will Give You Chills," BuzzFeed News, March

2, 2018, buzzfeednews.com/article/davidmack/little-girl-michelle
-obama-portrait.

Five Wishes of Wonder for This One Life

Todd Rose and Ogi Ogas, *Achieving Success Through the Pursuit of
Fulfillment* (New York: HarperOne, 2018).

Rachel Carson, "Help Your Child to Wonder," *Woman's Home
Companion*, July 1956, 25–27, 46–48.

ABOUT THE AUTHOR

JEFFREY DAVIS WORKS WITH innovators, professionals, writers, scientists, and social psychologists, offering him leading insights into the creative process. He is a sought-after speaker who presents at conferences, universities, and centers nationwide. Founder of Tracking Wonder Consultancy, he works with organizations and individuals to advance their best ideas and best lives with integrity and wonder. He lives with his family in the Hudson Valley of New York.

ABOUT SOUNDS TRUE

SOUNDS TRUE IS A multimedia publisher whose mission is to inspire and support personal transformation and spiritual awakening. Founded in 1985 and located in Boulder, Colorado, we work with many of the leading spiritual teachers, thinkers, healers, and visionary artists of our time. We strive with every title to preserve the essential "living wisdom" of the author or artist. It is our goal to create products that not only provide information to a reader or listener but also embody the quality of a wisdom transmission.

For those seeking genuine transformation, Sounds True is your trusted partner. At SoundsTrue.com you will find a wealth of free resources to support your journey, including exclusive weekly audio interviews, free downloads, interactive learning tools, and other special savings on all our titles.

To learn more, please visit SoundsTrue.com/freegifts or call us toll-free at 800.333.9185.

sounds true
WAKING UP THE WORLD